a Reliable Witness

How to give credible
mental health evidence
in court

By
Phil Watts
Ogilvie Publishing

A Reliable Witness: how to give credible evidence in court.

Copyright © Dr Philip Watts, 2004
This book is copyright. Apart from that permitted under the *Copyright Act 1968 (Cwlth)*, no portion can be reproduced or copied in any form, or by any means, without prior written permission from the author.

Ogilvie Publishing
PO Box 1084
Canning Bridge, 6153
Western Australia

Editing by Final Edits of Mt Lawley
Cover design by Worldwide Online Printing of Applecross
Typesetting by Artype Productions
Indexing by Linda McNamara
Printed by Artproof Printing Company of North Fremantle

Watts, Phil, 1962- .
A reliable witness.

1st ed.
Bibliography.
Includes index.
ISBN 0 9756042 0 1.

1. Evidence, Expert - Australia. 2. Witnesses - Australia. 3. Examination of witnesses - Australia. 4. Mental health personnel - Legal status, laws, etc. - Australia. I. Title.

347.94067

ACKNOWLEDGMENTS

Anyone who has ever written a book knows that is the product of much help and encouragement. I would like to thank the psychologists who have helped me understand the complexity of psychological assessment for court, in particular, Ross Smith, Ge Van Ireland and Russell Bailey-Brookes.

A special thanks to the following people of the legal profession who have taught me about the art of appearing in court including Kate Stockwell, Karen Farley, Donna Webb, Lucy Thomas, John Pacy, John Athanasiou, Julia Johnston, Sarah Tovey and Frank Castiglione, to mention some of the notable influences. I also acknowledge the judges of the courts who through their judgments have given me knowledge about how evidence is perceived in court.

Two barristers, Steven Jones and David Childs, kindly provided constructive criticism of this book. I am deeply appreciative of their 'insider' perspective being added to my professional understanding. Similarly, I am grateful for the assistance of Oleh Kay, psychiatrist, and Anna Fagence, forensic psychologist, in helping to put these ideas into perspective.

The idea of developing a training seminar into print form came from Michael and Leslie Tunnecliffe. I thank them for their inspiration, encouragement and practical help as I would never have considered taking on the task. I was encouraged by

Leonie Coxon, Jan Steel and Cris DeRooster to believe in myself and to develop the book.

A special thanks to my loving wife Bethwyn for her unending support and to my delightful children Jarom and Arielle who inspire me to be a better person.

CONTENTS

IMPORTANT NOTES & DISCLAIMERS vii

FOREWORD ix

INTRODUCTION – THE 'GAME' OF COURT 1
Law and Government 3
The Rules of the 'Game' 6

1 – PATHWAYS TO COURT 13
The Forensic Expert 15
Treatment Provider Issues 23
Negligence 36
Risk Management 43

2 – WRITING REPORTS FOR COURT 51
Key Principles in Report Writing 52
Structure of Reports 67

3 – THE RELIABLE WITNESS 78
The Reliable Witness 78
Process of Testing the Evidence 81
Communication with Lawyers 89
Rules of Evidence 92
Expert Evidence 96
Acting as a Reliable Witness 100

4 – GOING TO COURT 103
Court Dates and Times 103
Giving Evidence 106
Court Room Procedures 111
Costing 117
Becoming a Better Expert 120
Learning from My Mistakes 123
Final Advice 128

APPENDIX JUDGE WISBEY – PAPER 129

INDEX 137

REFERENCE LIST & FURTHER READING 143

NOTES 146

ABOUT THE AUTHOR 151

IMPORTANT NOTES AND DISCLAIMERS

In preparing this book, I am aware that there is a gap in the available Australian literature. There is information about giving evidence in court provided by lawyers which is legally correct but does not properly take into account the subtleties of the health profession. Such literature is technically correct but often tedious or irrelevant to mental and other health professionals. This is especially the case because most non-lawyers do not understand the legal narrative. There are also books written by academics in the mental health area which are extremely useful in a technical sense but for the busy professional, seem dry and irrelevant.

This book is written by an experienced forensic psychologist, which means although I understand the mental health profession, I may not necessarily have a full legal understanding of the legal subtleties. It is also written to be a practical guide, rich with personal experience. As such, I stress the following three cautions:

1. This book is designed to provide generic advice. It is important to realise that protocols vary between different

courts, States and areas of law. If you go to the Family Court, District Court, Supreme Court, or the Court of Petty Sessions there are both commonalities and individual differences. The better you understand the particular environment, the better you will perform and the more credible you will appear. Please ensure you seek local advice about your particular forum to supplement the general details contained in this book.

2. I am not a lawyer and this book is not giving you legal advice. What I am offering, however, are observations and experiences I have found useful in a court context. They are carefully considered but not infallible. If in doubt, seek a legal opinion before acting on the material in this book. Legal opinions are relatively easy to come by. The *Yellow Pages* and the local law societies will readily refer you to lists of legal professionals willing to help. However, like the advice from any profession, make sure the person you deal with has the necessary competence and expertise in the particular area of law relevant to your issues.

3. Different mental health professions have ethical standards which increasingly specify particular approaches to legal issues. For example, in the discussion on treatment provider issues in chapter one, it is mentioned that caution should be used not to blur the boundaries between assessment and treatment. This is consistent with *APS Code of Ethics (1999)*. The *RANZCP (2003) guideline 9* takes a firmer position by explicitly advising that psychiatrists should not provide routine treatment to patients referred for medical examinations except in exceptional circumstances. A second example is in regards to changing your report at the request of a lawyer. In chapter two I discuss the circumstances where I would amend a report. Under guideline 9 of the RANZCP (2003) it states that a report must never be amended but supplementary reports can be prepared. I strongly encourage you to study and always follow the guidelines of your association over and above any recommendations I provide in this book.

FOREWORD

Most health professionals dislike court. This varies from feelings of disdain due to the disruption of their normal routines through to absolute terror at the prospect of being critically examined in what is essentially an alien environment. The part of the legal process most professionals want to avoid is actually being in court and having to give expert evidence. While often seen as an inconvenience, most do not mind the report writing.

What most professionals fail to adequately understand is that the credibility of the evidence is not just the result of how they appeared in court on the day. While that is certainly a factor of great significance, much of the process is shaped by the position taken in the report they have already prepared. Likewise, the position to be taken in the report will be influenced by the way the professional deals with the initial contact from the lawyer. It is the position taken at the beginning which shapes how the report is written and the evidence is given. This is the critical factor which is going to influence the sort of cross-examination you will receive at the trial.

This book is designed to be a practical guide which helps to explain each step of the legal process for the health professional.

The structure of the book loosely follows the process which leads someone into court. The first chapter examine ways in which you may get drawn into the court system and how this influences the structure of the report provided. The second chapter examines some of the issues in writing reports for court as this is the basis of the evidence which can be given. The third chapter presents a model or schema of how an expert needs to be perceived by the court. This is something I have developed over my years of experience in court and dealing with lawyers. Once mastered, you will never view court in the same way again and you increase the likelihood of being perceived as a reliable witness. The final chapter is a practical guide which covers some of the 'how to' aspects of giving evidence in court.

INTRODUCTION – THE 'GAME' OF COURT

As you start dealing with legal professionals, you will suddenly find yourself transported to another world. Within this alien world, you will find that they use words of a familiar language in different ways, as well as use terms of a different language. Things which make common sense and seem obvious are overlooked while, at other times, procedures become bogged down with strange rules and apparently petty details. Part of the message this book hopes to convey is that the differences between health professionals and lawyers can be understood. It is designed to teach you about some of the subtle (and not so subtle) differences in communication and rules. In therapy jargon, lawyers use a different narrative in their communication processes to health professionals.

I found this out by chance rather than through any particular learning process. This came about when I was a new graduate, full of enthusiasm and naivety. My first job was working in a juvenile detention centre. One of my main tasks was to write reports for the Children's Court. After writing these reports they would be sent off in a manila envelope to an entity called 'court'. Every now and then I was asked to go along and give evidence. When I had to appear in court it was terrifying. My early experience of appearing in court was that two seemingly very hostile people were trying to rip me to pieces while a stern-looking judge alternated between frowning and looking bored throughout the process. At the end of it all, I would feel incredibly humiliated and would slither out on my belly, feeling lower than I ever thought possible. It terrified me! I think it terrifies most other professionals too because in our professional lives we are used to having our opinions and views respected and not critically challenged.

One day I was in the Children's Court and two lawyers were having their usual go at me. The twist in this case was that the lawyer who was cross-examining me happened to be a close friend. Something about the court environment had turned this normally compassionate person into a vicious assailant ripping me to pieces! When she finished, the prosecutor, a police officer, also tried to rip holes in my evidence. After they had ended their attacks upon me, I tried to make a hasty exit as the court adjourned for lunch. My friend then came over and said: "Phil, do you want to come to lunch?" As a result of my recent experiences, I may have thought, "with you! Not in this life!" Instead I politely smiled and said: "Oh sure, I would love to". Then she said to the prosecutor: "Do you want to come too?"

Herein lies the apparent irony of the legal system. There we were, chatting together over lunch when moments before we had been at each other in the most serious of situations. That was when I realised that court is in some ways like a game. It is very serious 'game' with big decisions being considered. It is very ego-threatening when you are not used to the rules, but it has some characteristics of a game nonetheless. As a result of this experience, I set about trying to understand how this process works and its inherent rules. In my opinion, it is as critical that you understand the rules as it is to have done a good assessment, whether clinically or using the tests of your profession. Prior to explaining the rules, it is important to briefly understand why court systems exist in every modern society.

Law and Government

Under the Australian Constitution there are three separate streams of power. These are legislative power which is the Parliament, executive power which is constitutionally under the Governor General, and the judicial power. Most people in Australia know that the demarcation between the legislative and executive power is somewhat blurred as the Governor General rarely acts in an independent capacity (the functional executive is made up of Ministers who are also members of the party or coalition of parties which holds a majority of seats in the House of Representatives). Therefore, although the Constitution clearly delineates three streams of power, the practical reality is that for most purposes there are only two separate streams which are the government and judiciary. As far as I am aware, most democratic societies have the law and government as separate bodies. The purpose of having the two streams of power is to ensure the good order of the country for the benefit of all people. The separation of law and government prevents the ruling body from enacting their own rules which are constitutionally inappropriate. Further more, individuals have rights but government and law place limits for the good of the majority.

Sections 71–80 of the Australian Constitution give the provisions for the creation of a High Court, and then specify the roles and powers of that body. Brian McNamara, in his book *How Australia is Governed* (1999, p. 36) states: "The High Court is the supreme court of the country and its decisions must be accepted by everyone, including governments". It is quite profound to think that a decision must be accepted by everyone irrespective of what they may want or believe. To cause all people to obey, law has to have a set of rules powerful enough to ensure that this happens. A simple implication is that requests for written or oral information by a court, called a subpoena, are very difficult not to comply with since the court needs information for the good of all people. A subpoena is backed up by large penalties to ensure it is fulfilled when and how the court requires the information.

The role of the High Court's function is to interpret the rules of the country which were created by the government. This process results in laws being made by the government, which the courts use to make their decisions. If someone does not like the way a rule was interpreted, it is appealed and eventually the High Court may hear the appeal as it is the highest court in Australia. Even laws made by State governments can be appealed in the High Court. Therefore, over time there are two types of law present in the system. There is the written law (statutes) as well as the way law has been successively interpreted by courts (case law). Often just reading the legislation or statutes will not be sufficient enough to understand the application. It is how successive judges have interpreted the law, especially when the decisions have been appealed and heard by courts of high authority, which provide the true understanding of the law.

In the most basic terms, law is the application of a set of rules to a dispute. This dispute could be between a couple resulting in Family Court action, two members of the public resulting in civil action, between an individual and the community resulting in various actions such as in the criminal court, or some other conflict between parties. The rules applied are based on written and case law peculiar to each area. As a community we want law to be based on fairness. However, a court can only make a decision on the application of the rules, the fairness has to have been written into the laws by the government. Therefore, someone getting let off a serious crime on a 'technicality' is essentially a problem with the way the rules were written, not necessarily the way the court applied them. Law can only apply the rules.

Within the structure of court there are various models which can be applied. The two most commonly seen approaches are the adversarial and inquiry methods. The adversarial approach, commonly seen in criminal and civil courts of Australia, has two or more sides. A neutral party, either a judge or jury, hears the fact and decides on an outcome after the sides of the case have been presented. The best evidence is deemed to win in the case of competing parties, or is deemed to have passed (or failed to pass) the standard of proof in other cases, particularly criminal matters. The judge also has the role of ensuring the case is presented according to legal requirements.

The inquiry method is commonly seen in tribunals and other bodies. The role of the judge is to find out information and make a decision. Some courts may have aspects of both, or the same court may use different systems in different States. For example, the functioning of a children's court may be based on the adversarial model or it may have powers of inquiry depending on the State. Similarly, the Family Court was set up to be inquisitorial but it still has a strong adversarial aspect. From a health professional's perspective, the experience is likely to feel the same but there are subtle differences, for example, a judge may ask you more questions in the Family Court.

The Rules of the 'Game'

Throughout this book, I use the analogy of court being a game. Below I outline some of the 'rules' of the game as relevant from a witness's perspective. However, prior to describing these rules, I would like to qualify certain aspects of the analogy. A game implies that there are two willing sides playing and that one will win. In court, one side may not be a willing party and often both sides will end up with substantial losses, both emotionally and financially. I am yet to hear both sides of a marriage break-up come out of the Family Court trial reporting that they were happy with the decision! On the other hand, like a game there are clearly defined rules which you need to know if you want to be successful. Similarly, your performance is an important determinant in the outcome.

For the judicial readers, my intention is not to demean the legal process by this analogy. The purpose is to help explain an alien environment from a framework that makes sense from the typical non-legal professional's perspective. A point I emphasise to all readers is that court is among the most serious and formal forums of our modern society. It needs to be treated with respect and dignity.

There are various rules of court. Those relevant to the 'game' of court from the perspective of the outsider are the following:

1. Court is fair, efficient and speedy.
2. Legal decisions are based on the appearance of truth.
3. Favourable evidence is that which is the more believable of two sides.
4. It does not matter what you did, it only matters what you can prove you did.

Each of these four rules are now discussed in detail below.

Rule 1 – Court is fair, efficient and speedy.

Anyone who has been involved in the legal arena is probably laughing after reading this rule. Court is not about the concept of fairness as a lay person understands fairness; it is about law. As described above, law is about a set of rules which were made and enacted in Parliament and became legislation. Since the rules were formulated, they have been used in court. Judges interpret these rules and people appeal decisions. These appeals are questioned by higher courts. The process of interpreting and appealing interpretations results in case law. Therefore, over time, the rules written in the legislation become tested by case law. The tested cases become the measure by which all legal decisions are made until new legislation is enacted. It becomes a system of logic which is about applying rules to making decisions. This may seem like a strange concept but when you grasp it, it makes dealing with the legal system much easier to understand.

Lawyers will generally see the rules of court as being fair. For example, hearsay rules exist to prevent information being used in court which may be of questionable source. However, from a witness point of view, if you were told something but were not allowed to rely on it in court, it would seem very unfair. Consequently, community perception of the unfairness of court exists because of the different systems of logic. As a member of the community the more you can understand law as a set of rules applied to a dispute, the easier it is to accept the various anomalies in apparent fairness.

The second part of rule one is that the court is efficient and speedy. Like the court being fair, this is also a fallacy due to misunderstandings and certain practical realities. The court process takes some time to run its course. In my travels around Australia presenting seminars on this topic, I have found surprisingly similar timeframes. In Western Australia and in other jurisdictions, a typical criminal matter of a more serious nature, if the offender pleads not guilty, will take somewhere between 12 and 18 months from when they were charged to when they are sentenced after the trial.

A typical civil matter such as a workers' compensation claim, negligence, or motor vehicle accident claim will take anywhere from about two to ten years to settle, unless there is a separate system which streamlines the process (such as in worker's compensation). If you work with children in these areas, it may be well over a decade before that case runs to trial. For example, a neurologist specialising in assessing children's head injuries who does an assessment on a eight year old injured in a car accident, may find themselves in court a decade later as the lawyers may not even consider settling the case until that child is nearly an adult. The report that the professional completed in 2004, based on three or four hours of assessment, may not go to trial until 2014!

In the Family Court, if a complex matter involving serious allegations is resolved by trial in less than 12 months then something unusual seems to have happened! It generally takes one to three years from the initial application to when the matter is decided by a trial. For average matters, it is currently around 12 months from start to trial and can be quicker in expedited trials. An added complication in the Family Court is that particular issues may settle but children remain. Matters which were resolved can resurface years later with new issues. Generally these are the more serious cases, but it is not uncommon to have files which were first in court up to ten years ago. From the health practitioner's perspective, any child you have seen in your practice may end up in a Family Court dispute and you could be required to provide information of importance to the trial, even though a particular child was seen years ago.

For the client, there are advantages and disadvantages to the long timeframes. The main advantage is that people may not be stable enough to settle early. For example, it takes one or two years to grieve the loss of a major relationship so early settlement in the Family Court may not reflect the long-term best interests of the parties. Similarly, time is required for injuries to stabilise. Some of the disadvantages of long timeframes for the client include the fact that people may not progress while there are secondary gains from not getting better, the stress of court is extremely high, and the longer legal matters run the greater the potential to accrue massive legal debt.

For the professional having to appear in court, long timeframes seem to hold no special advantages beyond the opportunity to collect more information. The implication of the slow timeframe is that when you are taking case notes and writing your report, you need to do it in such a way that, in two or three years time, your notes have sufficient information to allow you to give credible evidence, even if you do not specifically remember the case!

Rule 2 – Legal decisions are based on the appearance of truth.

To understand this second point, it is important to consider that when whatever event happened to result in court action, the judge, applicant's lawyer, respondent's lawyer nor the jury were present. However, these are the people who are running the process or making the decisions. The judge and jury can only listen to the witnesses who come along to give evidence and form views about what really happened. They look at the appearance of truth, because they do not have access to the absolute truth.

The way they assess the appearance of truth is by accessing at the credibility of the witnesses, both ordinary and expert. They also examine documents and tangible evidence to corroborate the different sources of information in a logical whole. The lawyers try to highlight or discredit the believability – reliability – of witnesses and other evidence to show which version of the facts is most plausible and consistent. It is not about finding an absolute truth as in most cases there is no direct discovery of the absolute truth. Flowing from this is the importance of both your personal presentation and the presentation of your evidence as critical factors in the court environment.

Rule 3 – Favourable evidence is that which is the more believable of two sides.

Following on from rule 2 is, that after carefully observing the evidence given by the witnesses, the judge gains some understanding of what is apparently true. The judge has to decide what he or she believes from the arguments heard and evidence presented. He or she decides the truth based on whom and what was the more believable of the two sides. The process of reaching a conclusion from the available evidence and then applying the relevant law to those findings allows the judicial officer to come to a decision or judgment about a particular matter.

In making the judgment, the judge has to justify the conclusions based on forensic logic and will go through the evidence heard or seen and will make comments about how important or 'material' the evidence appeared. The judge is obliged to give reasons for his or her decision. In doing this the judge may say: "I find Dr Jones a reliable witness" or "I find Dr Jones an unreliable witness". Sometimes they will give a qualified position such as "I think Dr Jones was a reliable witness but I think he overstated this point or put too much weight on that evidence". Through this process, the judge justifies the decision and decides on which position was more acceptable.

Rule 4 – It does not matter what you did, it only matters what you can prove you did.

To reach a judgment, the evidence is assessed for credibility, and if credible, accorded with significant weight. This is where your records become important. Once you are in the witness box, you need to prove your position. Just knowing you did something is not enough. It becomes a question of your word against someone else's position. The court will find your position more credible if you have handwritten contemporaneous notes or recordings, so you can prove what actually happened to a greater degree of certainty. To be able to use them in court, you have to argue the link between the notes or test results and the relevance to your evidence. Lawyers may talk about this principle in terms of the 'best evidence' rule.

The process you use to record your evidence will be examined closely. One recent experience stems from the fact that when a client is talking, although I am writing down what are they are saying, I sometimes do not manage to record all of it. I know what the person is telling me but if I do not have it in my notes I have a problem. In a particular Family Court case, a Queen's Counsel (QC) asked: "Is this what the person told you?" followed by, "can you show me where in your notes he said that?" Had I said: "The person talks faster than I can record" the QC would have said, "so your notes are not reliable, are they Dr Watts?" The message here is the better your records, the better you will survive the court experience.

1

PATHWAYS TO COURT

It is essential to understand that the credibility of your evidence depends on how you structure your role from the beginning. It makes a lot of difference which pathway brings you into court. As I see it, there are three main pathways to court.

The first is the forensic expert. Forensic experts are those like me who actively seek work within the legal arena knowing that there is a real possibility of having to give evidence in court on the information collected. At the time of writing this book, there were nearly 500 registered clinical psychologists and yet there are only about 20 registered forensic psychologists in Western Australia. This shows how many within my profession like working within the legal arena. In talking to GPs and other professionals, I find a similar ratio.

A second pathway brings those professionals providing treatment of some type, and do not actively seek court work, into the court arena. One day you are peacefully doing your work and then a subpoena lands on your desk. It demands that you please attend court. Alternatively a lawyer rings you up and says: "I need a report for my client who is your patient; will you provide one?" I particularly wrote this book for those of you who come into court via this second pathway.

A third way you could end up being drawn into the court system as a professional is through negligence claims. This is the least desirable position to be in. In the situation of negligence you are personally on the line because you have either done something wrong or have been accused of doing something wrong.

I have not included miscellaneous life experiences which may draw all people into court. For example, if you were banking the business takings and witnessed a robbery, you may well be called to give evidence. However, your evidence will be as a lay witness, not as a professional or expert witness. In this case, you will only be giving evidence of fact, which is evidence of what you have seen and heard.

I have not included the pathway to court which is initiated by the actions of an investigative professional. Workers in a child protection capacity may conduct investigations which are for the purpose of determining whether a child has been abused. These cases initiate the legal proceedings rather than provide evidence to existing proceedings. In this type of case, although they are professional witnesses, their most important information will usually be the evidence of fact generated from their investigations. Opinions will be considered but are secondary factors.

In the following sections, each of these areas will be discussed in detail. Although the majority of readers will be treatment providers rather than forensic experts, it is important to structure your approach like a forensic expert. In my opinion, it is of crucial importance that you understand the principles which underlie how the forensic expert conducts their practice, if you are going to survive the court system.

The Forensic Expert

There is a hierarchy of levels in which a forensic expert can be appointed in the system. The following list varies from the most desirable to least desirable position in terms of the perceived strength of your evidence:

Court-appointed Expert

Agreed Expert

Party Expert

Paper Expert

Second Opinion Expert

Court-appointed Expert

Under various Acts of Parliment, courts can have the ability to appoint their own expert. The Family Court uses many experts and they will regularly appoint mental health professionals to talk to children and/or assess parents. Other courts may have the capacity to appoint an expert but in Western Australia, as in other States, it is an option which is rarely used except in the case of children's courts. One recent exception, which I am aware of, was a negligence case. It involved a neuropsychological assessment. Two of my colleagues had assessed a client and had given evidence in court. One side was for the plaintiff and the other for the insurance company. The judge said: "I need another opinion", so he appointed a colleague to be a third opinion. The judge said he would accept that third opinion. He appointed an independent psychologist over and above the parties who had already been retained.

If it is possible for you to be appointed as the court expert in a matter, it is the strongest position to be in because you are actually classed as an officer of the court. You are working for the court so your role is seen as neutral and independent. The position of independence is a decided advantage at the start of your evidence. You may still be seen as biased at the end of your evidence, but that would be due to your approach and presentation, not the role. As will be explained in Chapter 3, your ability to be seen as independent and not influenced by a particular bias, determines how credible the court perceives you to be. In other words, the protection afforded by the role of court expert is limited by the degree your biases influence your evidence.

One of the ironies of this is that by being more involved with the court you are less likely to have to give evidence. I have been appointed as court expert in close to 300 Family Court matters in Western Australia. Less than one in ten of these messy, complex family assessments ends up in trial. Why? Because I am independent to both the parties involved and the judiciary place some significance on my views. Where I get asked to assess a parent only, about 50 per cent of these cases end up in trial. Why? I may be seen as working for one side and my evidence is not given as much weight, so the parties do not reach agreement.

Agreed Expert

The next level of independence is the agreed expert. Two opposing parties may ask to have you provide an independent assessment without a court order to legitimate the role. Here you may have your independence but you are no longer an officer of the court. I find this tends to occur when lawyers know my work and they know each other.

A simple example of how to do this is when a lawyer for a father in the family court rings up and says: "Do you want to do an assessment of my client?" You can say, "no, but I will do an assessment of your client, the mother and the child". They ring the mother's lawyer and now you are an agreed expert with a greater degree of independence. Your evidence as an independent party is much stronger than evidence which you would have given in the other role, the party expert.

Party Expert

A party expert is someone who agrees to work for one party to provide a report. Someone wants an opinion and they have asked you for it. The problem with this is that you are likely to be seen as either biased by the court, or lacking in counter information to reach a balanced view. You may be the most independent practitioner in the world, but because you have just worked for one side, you may be seen by the court as having a bias.

It is important to manage that process of your appointment to maximise usefulness. There are many subtle ways of doing this. One example is through a request to be subpoenaed. While subpoenas are discussed in more detail later, an example is as follows. Previously, I did a Family Court expert assessment where I was the court expert and the father involved had been convicted for some assaults which were extremely violent. He had taken his former defacto at gunpoint up into the hills, sexually and physically assaulted her, and was threatening to kill her before she managed to escape. He was eventually gaoled but after his release he went around to her house and did the same thing again, but this time with a knife. Obviously, this was someone with significant pathology of risk. When I did the Family Court assessment I concluded that there should not be any contact between this man and the child for various reasons. Several years later the woman approached me to give evidence at a restraining order hearing as the former partner was to be paroled. I said I was willing to appear in court but requested that she subpoena me. Why the subpoena? If I had gone along as her witness, then I may have been seen as biased, and because I had collected the evidence as a court expert, I may have run into confidentiality issues. As I was subpoenaed I could go to court and keep the role as court expert, for example I could say: "I didn't do this assessment for her, Your Honour, I did it for the Family Court as a court expert and this is what I found…" I had now moved from being a party expert to a role almost as independent as the court-appointed expert.

If you are going to work as a party expert, it is important to acknowledge your limitations. What the court needs to know is the basis of your evidence. Highlight any significant limitations to your evidence. It is important to say: "I have seen X but I have not seen Y". It is also important to state documents you read or people you interviewed. If you go to court and a lawyer says, "you did not see Y, did you?" and you say "no" and they say, "well, should you?" you can say, "I have outlined in my report why I did not". The court is then in a position to determine that you have done your job carefully and considered options knowing you lacked certain pieces of information.

Paper Expert

For want of a better name, a paper expert is someone who offers a theoretical view on a topic but generally does not see anyone. It is a theoretical opinion only – a dry academic review. It does not matter what area you specialise in – it might as be as obscure as people's phobic reactions to pigeons – sooner or later some lawyer will want an expert opinion on phobic reactions to pigeons. They will ask around your colleagues until they find someone, whether a clinician or an academic researcher, who can answer the questions they need answering. Some examples of where I have offered paper expert opinion to the Family Court include giving opinions about the capability of homosexual men to parent, Battered Wife Syndrome, whether Post-Traumatic Stress Disorder really exists (although with the *DSM-IV* that is a reasonably easy one to argue), and the theoretical ages when children best cope with overnight contact.

There are several major issues to consider in offering opinions on a topic in isolation. The first is to make sure that you really are an expert in the subject before you offer the opinion. Secondly, make sure you clearly spell out your limitations in the report. Thirdly, stay within the bounds of what you know and do not speculate into other areas. If you are careful to stay within the bounds of your expertise, the information provided may be of vital importance to the court. On the other hand, paper opinions may be perceived as having no substance.

I had an interesting example where a lawyer rang up and asked if I could provide a critique of an article from America which offered some theoretical criteria used to determine whether someone had sex offender characteristics. After I reviewed the article he asked if I would assess his client against the criteria. Unfortunately, the client matched every one of the theoretic risk factors! I had to contact the briefing lawyer and state my position along the lines that if I provided a report it would not be of any use to the case as a defence. I ended up providing a pre-sentence report when the man was convicted of the offences.

Second Opinion Expert

A second opinion expert is someone who provides an opinion on another professional's report (this is not to be confused with a genuine second opinion which is actually a party expert because they have seen the client in real life for one side of the dispute). The original professional has written a report based on an assessment and then you examine it to offer a theoretical review of the strengths and weaknesses of the assessment and report. Taking such a role means that the court may see you as both biased and limited because you have not assessed anybody. All you are doing is commenting on how your colleague went about the task.

There is a place for this type of review but be aware of the potential problems. It is not a time to get personal or promote a particular agenda. It is essential that you focus on such aspects as the methodology, the approach, the logic in the other professional's reasoning, and whether their findings are reasonable. Do not get into making statements like, "this person is an idiot and does not know what they are talking about". Do not engage in personal attacks, nor criticise their areas of expertise – base the critique on the content and process, not the person. This approach is important not only for reasons of professional courtesy but also because an attack on another professional tends to weaken your own credibility.

If your report is critiqued, consider carefully whether you should even respond. The natural inclination may be to write a detailed rebuttable. All that does is to provide the lawyers with ammunition to use against you. Once, I went away for five weeks and on my return found three critiques of different comprehensive assessments I had conducted as court expert. I took the first very seriously and in my stressed state I wrote something like 25 pages in response to the criticism. I was advised by another lawyer not to respond to the other two. Instead, I wrote a simple response which said: "I do not think the criticisms are valid and I am willing to address them at trial". As a strategy it worked well in that particular case. Please note that I received legal advice before acting. In a different situation, another strategy may have been warranted.

Another approach is, rather than offering a second opinion critique, I sometimes provide lawyers with a cross-examination strategy. Lawyers may find this useful as they often do not understand mental health concepts or medical terminology. This approach helps them understand what the professional is saying. At times I have been amazed at the lack of understanding a lawyer may have about a medical report. For example, I had a case where the lawyers read a neuropsychological report and did not realise it said the person had brain damage from an acquired injury. In this role, I interpret what the professional is saying and highlight the strengths and weaknesses of the report. Lawyers can find that very useful while colleagues may not.

If you are going to prepare a second opinion report, make sure you find out whether you are actually allowed to see the report. Certain courts have rules about their reports. I was involved in a case where I wrote a report for the Family Court. My report was sent by the father to a colleague to do a critique and see the children. The second psychologist was not familiar with the intricacies of the Family Court. When he went to give evidence at the trial, the judge sternly berated him because he had read the report without permission from the court and he had seen the children when a court order prevented them from being seen by another professional without the approval of the court. Ignorance of these matters will be no defence before a judge. In regards to the Family Court of Australia, anyone preparing material should be familiar with Part 15 of the *Family Law Rules* which refers to expert evidence. Other courts will have relevant rules pertaining to particular protocol. Procedures and rules for most courts can be downloaded from the Internet.

If in doubt about the rules for releasing reports, there are some simple strategies to adequately address consent issues. If a client wants to give you a report directly, refuse, and request that their lawyer send it to you. It would be assumed by the court that the lawyer should have obtained the necessary permissions. When I write these reports, I often state: "This report was provided by such and such solicitor. I assume they have the necessary releases for me to have seen the report". Who does the judge blame now if there are problems? The lawyer will be the one who is more likely to receive any criticism, not the professional.

I avoid having the client give me documents for several reasons. Sometimes clients will give documents which are considered very prejudiced or which you should not be seeing. In one case, in the middle of my evidence, I made a passing comment that I had seen a particular document. The judge immediately stopped the trial. I was then sent out of the court while they debated whether or not I should have seen the document. At the end of the debate they decided I should not have seen it and disqualified all of my evidence. The moral here is to be very careful what information you use and how you get it. Most of the time, it will not be a problem but be cautious in your approach as there are intricacies in rules of evidence that can affect you. On the other hand, not having seen particular evidence may jeopardise the usefulness of your evidence so it is important not to ignore useful information because of concerns about admissibility.

Forensic Expert and Personal Risk

The final point to consider with the forensic expert role is to understand that if you are going to work in this area you are often working with clients who may be disturbed, highly stressed and/or very angry. In simple terms, reasonable people usually solve their problems without having to go to court so in the legal arena some of the people have pathologies which make them unreasonable. This includes personality disorders, certain intellectual or cognitive limitations, mental illnesses, and so forth. They may have been convicted of violent acts in the past or have significant stress from being in the legal system. A few of those are also still very dangerous. Personally, I have not had death threats but one of my colleagues had a man visit his office and threaten to kill him, and another colleague was murdered. While considering your risk, it is important not to lose sight of the fact that there are many socially appropriate and reasonable people who need help so do not assume all are bad.

It is important to structure your practice in a way which considers the possibility that some of your clients may have psychological and other disturbances. I have a home office which I use on a limited basis but the main consulting rooms are elsewhere. I would not do any criminal or Family Court assessment from the home office because it is too risky. I only see those clients in the home office who have been carefully screened.

Treatment Provider Issues

Any professional giving evidence needs to understand the principles which have been discussed for the forensic expert. The principles are directly relevant to being a credible witness. However, for the professional whose practice is about providing treatment, not specifically assessments for court, there are other issues and pathways to court to consider. As a treatment provider, you are doing what you are trained to do, that is, to provide some type of service which was not necessarily intended to have a legal purpose. However, out of the blue a client may request a report, the client's lawyer rings you up and wants a report, a subpoena is delivered to your office, or there is some other means for thrusting your treatment information into the legal system.

Sometimes lawyers use cunning means. For example, most lawyers understand that health providers hate going to court. They find that if they ring up and say: "I have a client I want you to see for treatment so you can give us a report for court", they get the answer, "no thanks, we do not do legal work, send them to somebody else". Being clever, the lawyers have cottoned on to that. They then use different strategies such as this one which came in a recent letter to me. The letter's first sentence read: "We arranged for Donna to attend at your Mount Pleasant office on 19th December. As you may not be aware, we act for..." What they had done was send this lady to see me as a treating psychologist but with the deliberate intention of wanting a report. The Australian Psychological Society (APS) in New South Wales has an agreement between the New South Wales Legal Practitioners to try and stop this sort of conduct. I understand it was modelled on a similar approach between the Australian Medical Association (AMA) and the lawyers. I would be surprised if the backdoor approaches will stop completely for either profession although I have noted that such codes of practice appear to make some difference.

Being mindful that there are a variety of subtle ways which may end up drawing the treatment provider into court, the following represent the main pathways which will get you to court. Please note, unlike the forensic expert section which lists a hierarchy of preferred positions, the list below presents separate pathways which have no particular advantage of one over another:

Party Requested

Family Court

Subpoenas

Other Pathways

Before discussing the details of these pathways, it is worth commenting on the basic difference in position between that of a treatment provider and a forensic expert. The difference centres upon the awareness of the issues at question. As the forensic expert knows what questions are being asked, they have the luxury of conducting a comprehensive assessment which attempts to cover all main possibilities. The treatment provider collects information relevant to the treatment and may not have the knowledge to answer the question which the lawyer is interested in without having to see the client again.

Party Requested

The role of the party expert has been previously described. The difference here is that it is an existing or former client who is requesting information for the court, rather than beginning a new assessment with the particular issues of dispute in mind. The trouble with being requested by one of the parties in a legal dispute is that you may be seen as biased. You may be a good practitioner but there are pros and cons to entering the legal arena from that position. Some workers in the forensic mental health area argue about whether therapists should ever be called to give evidence. This is a loaded debate beyond the scope of this book but if you want to avoid legal pitfalls it is important that you think about some of the differences.

The obvious advantage of the treating professional giving evidence is that they see a client for a much longer period of time and get to know them better. The disadvantage is that they take on a sort of ownership of the patient and it gets very hard to be seen as independent not only to the court but to yourself. Another disadvantage is you may not have specifically examined the question the lawyer is asking of you. When in court, expect questions along the lines that you are biased, working for a particular person and other issues about your objectivity.

I have a mixed practice and I see clients for both treatment and forensic assessments. I would argue that I have different approaches to my forensic assessment and clinical work. I make a conscious effort to think differently. The mindset I have with a clinical client is I believe what they tell me, but I look for any inconsistencies and I give them feedback about these. If I am conducting a forensic assessment, I work from the position that I am sceptical about what they are telling me and I look for consistencies within the story and data. I do not give the client feedback during the assessment which is important as feedback may lead the client to respond in beneficial ways. In effect I am building a bottom-up picture for a forensic assessment, whereas in clinical practice I am doing a top-down process.

A different issue for the treating professional is the impact of the legal process on the therapeutic relationship. If you are treating someone and write a report on the client it can jeopardise how you get on in future sessions. I have had clients who have refused to come back and see me when I have put in writing my opinions. To explain, I might say to a client something along the lines of the following: "You have a long standing pattern of feeling very upset when people leave you so you get very distressed". They happily agree with the statement. In the legal report I write that "the client has a borderline personality disorder". After looking up the details on the Internet the client may never want to see me again. On the other hand, I have had a few clients come back and say I provided a great report and they are happy but, more often than not, they have ceased treatment or the relationship is strained.

There are ways you can deal with the process to maximise the chances of keeping the client-practitioner relationship functioning in a therapeutic way. One of the first things to do is find out whether the report is even needed. It is good practice to ring up the lawyer and explain some of these issues. The lawyer is interested in evidence but may be sensitive if you explain that you may not be able to help the client after the report is released. You can suggest a forensic assessment by someone else which may be more independent as you may be seen to be taking a biased position. If a lawyer believes you are biased, they will probably drop you like a hot potato. Too many health providers see a letter from a lawyer requesting a report and simply provide it without questioning the value of it with the lawyer.

Another approach which is useful is discussing the report with the client before you write it and going over the draft report before it is released. Being present to address issues often helps resolve the problem and prevent the client from misunderstanding the jargon, and also gives you a chance to explain your rationale. In this day and age of privacy legislation, it is critical that the client is aware of the report you write and that you have the necessary written permissions to release it.

Assuming you cannot negotiate out of the need for providing the report, the best guidance I can offer is to understand the difference between being a 'witness of fact' and an 'expert witness'. This point will be discussed later in the book but by way of introduction to the topic, a witness of fact can report what they have seen, heard or done. An expert opinion can comment on motive or reason for particular behaviour. As a treating professional, describing the symptom tends to be providing fact. The more you offer diagnosis and supposition for behaviour the further you go from fact and more into opinion. If in doubt, stick to fact and avoid opinion.

A final point of caution is about blurring the role between forensic assessment and clinical treatment in your practice. If providing treatment stick with treatment issues and recognise your limitations. If assessing, do not take the party on for treatment as this will significantly weaken any independence you gain by being in the role.

Family Court

The Family Court has to make decisions about complex family breakdowns which involve all sorts of problems – parents who cannot resolve their problems, concerns about the welfare of the children, issues surrounding domestic violence, drug treatment, intellectual difficulties, head injuries in accidents, psychiatric or medical illnesses, personality disorders, allegations of sexual abuse, or people who have come to the notice of major government departments for a variety of problems. Evidence from the agencies and professionals involved may help to shed light on the central issues of the case. For example, the interaction style noted by a therapist three years prior to a marital break-up may be critical in determining whether the current allegations of domestic violence are exaggerated for court or a well-documented problem of many years' duration.

Under the *Family Law Rules* introduced in early 2004, there is a clearly expressed difference between the court's expectations for a treating professional and an expert providing a report for the parties. If the treatment precedes the request for information and the information required is limited to evidence of facts about treatment or opinions solely about the treatment then Rule 15.5 of the Rules do not apply. If drawn into comments about parenting issues then the rules may apply. If the lawyer is talking to you about providing a report about non-treatment issues, to do an assessment of the parties, or you have not yet seen the parties, then the rule could well apply. Among the requirements are obligations for all communications between the lawyer and professional to be in writing, and that permission of the court may be needed before the information can be used. Therefore, immediately request written information from the lawyer and respond in writing. The situation is less obvious if the patient is self-represented. Ensure that you request written information as they may not be aware of the Rules.

In Western Australia, as in most States, there is a practice of subpoenaing any professional who may possibly have some information about the parties on their files. Whatever area of work you do, you are likely to find that you eventually will get a subpoena to produce evidence to the family court.

Subpoenas

A subpoena is a legal demand to provide information. It has a status similar to that of a court order. The court takes compliance with subpoenas very seriously. If the court cannot force people to meet its needs, then the constitutional independence of the legal system is threatened. Therefore, if you do not attend court or fail to get the subpoena put aside, a warrant for your arrest may be issued and you may be held in prison and brought to court on a day-by-day basis to give your evidence. This is of course an extreme example but it is coercive power the legal system has under law related to subpoena compliance.

In areas such as the Family Court, subpoenas are routine documents but still have to be taken seriously. If you are a 'friendly' witness the subpoena may just arrive in the mail after a request from a lawyer. In other cases it has to be 'served' on you. When it is served it has to be done in person and in a particular way.

The first thing to do when you get a subpoena is to read it carefully. Why do I say carefully? The subpoena may request an attendance in person or it might be just for documents. I have had colleagues attend court when all they needed to do was send documents. If the subpoena says on it 'DOCUMENTS' the file and any other requested documents go; if it says 'PERSON' then you have to attend (the issue of privileged information will be addressed later). If it states both, then you send the file and you also have to attend.

While subpoena law varies from State to State and from court to court, it is generally permissible to send a copy of the documents rather than the original. I received a subpoena from New South Wales recently in a workers' compensation matter. The subpoena specified a copy of my documents and provided photocopy money. In Western Australia, my last subpoena did not specify 'COPY' however upon investigation I was advised that copies were permissible. In some States or courts you might have to provide a Certified Copy so you go to a Justice of the Peace and swear they are original. In other cases, a copy with a letter saying 'I certify that this is an original copy' is enough. As repeated throughout this book, legal advice to find out the appropriate legal protocol is necessary. If you are unsure of what is required, find out from somebody who knows.

There are several reasons why I prefer to send a copy of documents. First of all, the Registry of the Court which receives the file will often hold it for a very long time. They may have the file for as long as 12 months or more. Imagine the situation where you have to go along to court to give evidence and you do not have your file. A second reason why I copy the file, especially in the family court, is that if you have the original you can see if someone has altered your notes. This is not common but I know of a case where one of the parties went through and actually changed some of details in a subpoenaed doctor's file. I often number the pages sequentially because the other thing which happens is sometimes whole pages go missing.

An interesting aspect of subpoena law is conduct money. This is something which may be specific to particular courts but by law when a subpoena is served they have to provide you with enough money to attend court (called conduct money). This rule is designed for general witnesses so they cannot use the excuse that they could not afford to get to court. For example, under the Family Law Rules (Schedule 4) a witness must be paid a minimum of $10 but the rule has provisions for accommodation, meals and return costs if over certain distances. However, if the conduct money is not provided when it is supposed to have been provided, then the subpoena may be deemed to have not been served correctly. In one particular case, I used this avenue to get out of attending court. However, I only did this with legal advice as it is a complex aspect of law with penalties if you get it wrong.

One of my colleagues thought that conduct money was all they could get paid. My understanding is that you can be paid a reasonable professional fee for complying with a subpoena over and above conduct money. For example, in the Family Court of Western Australia's provided information it states: "You may be entitled to recover reasonable costs incurred complying with a subpoena…You should advise the requesting party the estimated reasonable cost in writing as soon as possible. If there is a dispute, the court can be asked to make a ruling". With a New South Wales subpoena to produce documents for the District Court, I was sent a cheque for $25. They had a prescribed schedule of fees. In Western Australia we generally do not have a preset schedule for mental health professionals complying with subpoenas for most courts. Areas such as workers' compensation are generally the ones which are most likely to have prescribed fee schedules. If there is a dispute about payment, the court can make a ruling on what is a reasonable fee.

Generally the party who has subpoenaed you is the party who is responsible for the costs, whether they originally engaged your services or not. The legal profession has clearly defined rules and protocol for these types of issues but unless you know what they are, you have to ensure that you cover yourself. As a result, the first thing I do when I get a subpoena for attending court is write to the requesting party outlining what my reasonable costs are. Sometimes when the party is self-represented and they find out that they are responsible for costs they cancel the attendance. Once it is in writing, it is easier to argue that the fees were reasonable and agreed, if they are known prior to having given the evidence.

It is important to check the times and dates listed on the subpoena. A request for attendance in person is almost always worded in the legal equivalent to "9 am [or whatever time the court starts] on the first morning and day by day thereafter to the conclusion of trial". In reality, the court will almost never want you at 9 am on the first day as the lawyers have to run their opening arguments first (unless you are contesting the subpoena in which case they will want to hear these arguments before the trial commences in earnest). If you ring up the lawyer who subpoenaed you and ask when they will want you, they will usually be helpful in giving you an estimated time. They become even more helpful if you indicate that you charge the standard fee for the time available to the court. They will not want you sitting around for days at a charge of several hundred dollars per hour.

If you were not a professional being called as a witness, the chances are that the court may expect you to sit there from 9 am on the first day. The whole reason for this approach is that court is very expensive – judge, judge's associates, and a multitude of lawyers and barristers are all very costly to have waiting around for witnesses. Everything revolves around the court's convenience. They line up the witnesses outside the courtroom, so as soon as one is finished the next one can slot in, much like a production line. Therefore, they may request you at particular time but can only estimate when your slot in the production line will come up. As a professional person, if you talk to the briefing lawyer or trial barrister, in many cases they will interpose you. This means they put you in at an agreed time which is mutually convenient. In a four- or five-day trial, they work out roughly when they want you and you go in at the fixed time. It does not always happen on time, and you may still end up waiting, but it is very rare that I have had to spend more than half a day waiting at court.

Sometimes I am asked whether we need to get the details of a court attendance in writing. My experience is usually that verbal agreement is good enough but if you think you are dealing with Dodgy Brothers Solicitors Incorporated and you are suspicious about them, get it confirmed in writing. I do not find I have to be that paranoid as most of the lawyers I have dealt with are reasonable and fair.

I never make legal arrangements through the client unless they are self-represented. I never accept information from a client who says, "I spoke to my lawyer and you are needed on Wednesday". It is best to ring the lawyer. Sometimes I think health professionals are scared of talking to lawyers. If you ring, the lawyer is usually only too happy to talk to you. If they have subpoenaed you, you can say, "yes, I have got this information" or "no, I haven't". I was advising a friend recently who was subpoenaed by the opposing side to her client. My advice was to ring the subpoenaing lawyer and ask what information was wanted. She rang them and when she told them she did not have the required information they said for her to forget the subpoena. Of course she asked for a written confirmation that the subpoena had been cancelled.

There are certain limits to subpoenas. If the subpoena is 'onerous' you do not have to comply. How to define 'onerous' can be quite tricky and is a sign that legal advice is required. Once, I received a subpoena which asked for my case notes and "every article on parental alienation sent to me by the Legal Aid Commission of Western Australia". I wrote a letter back and stated I knew that Legal Aid had sent me some articles on parental alienation, but I did not know how many articles and said that they were in my general library of articles on family court issues. I sent in my clinical file and the letter after getting some legal advice. I never heard another word about it.

The timeframe is another limit to a subpoena. If the subpoena is issued within an unreasonable timeframe to comply, you may have grounds to not comply. You may want to have legal advice before you respond "you gave me only 24 hours so I did not comply". The other implication in not complying due to short timeframes is that the judge may not see you as being overly helpful to the court. Therefore, technically it may be sufficient not to comply but how will the judge assess you if you a) bent over backwards to comply, or b) held up court for months because they did not have your information?

A trap which is worth noting is complying on THREAT of subpoena. A lawyer may contact you along the following lines: "We are going to subpoena your notes, so can you send them to us now?" I had a colleague who did that, and she never actually received the subpoena. A very disgruntled, but ethically justified client may have had grounds to claim against the professional through both the Registration Board and Office of the Federal Privacy Commissioner who handle complaints under the *Privacy Amendment (Private Sector) Act 2000*. It is not the threat but the actual subpoena correctly served which is needed.

An original subpoena with the court stamp on it is important to keep on file. At the risk of generating unnecessary paranoia, I had a case once where a mother in a Family Court matter had cut, pasted and photocopied orders to make them read like the real orders but left out the bits which did not suit her! The bottom line is that you need to check what the local rules are for being correctly served a subpoena, as it will be you who will be held accountable if a dispute emerges.

In relation to confidentiality considerations under law, health professionals have a hard time arguing that information obtained from the client is confidential. Generally, it is not confidential. If trying to claim privilege, it is important to know that this is an area of complex law and legal advice is absolutely essential. However, there are areas where I have successfully argued for privilege of information. One was for the protection of psychological test material on the file. I argued that the validity of psychological tests can be damaged by public availability so I requested my psychological testing results only be released to another psychologist. The second was where I provided marriage counselling to a couple who subsequently separated. The husband had legal difficulties before the criminal court and wanted information from the file. The second party (wife) was no longer involved in the first person's life. I argued that reference to the second party was an unnecessary breach of confidentiality. This was upheld. Another area where confidentiality may be protected is for certain registered counsellors who provide counselling protected under the rules of an Act (discussed below).

It is important to consider copyright issues. Some material is copyrighted. For example, psychological tests and protocol sheets state on them that they are not to be photocopied. Seek advice before copying the material.

How privilege is structured varies depending on the court. In the marriage example just listed, I provided a complete set of my file notes in an envelope that was sealed and had 'Privilege' written on it. A copy of the notes with the privilege sections erased was placed in the main file for the court. On the first day of the trial a lawyer argued privilege for me. Had he failed, the court would open the envelope and made the notes available.

Some agencies and government departments are accorded privilege of information which is protected by Acts of Parliament. For example, around Australia certain types of counselling provided by Relationships Australia and other nominated agencies are protected from public scrutiny. If you work in these agencies your notes cannot be subpoenaed. However, information obtained in many other government departments such as welfare, education and health can be subpoenaed. The short answer is that if your work is in the public sector, check with your agency's legal section before acting on a subpoena.

Other Pathways

There are other main pathways which can lead to court or court-like bodies. There are bodies such as the Immigration Tribunal, Administrative Appeals Tribunal, Industrial Relations Commission, Guardianship and Administration Board, Workers' Compensation Board, Coroner's Court, Centrelink, and Environmental Courts, to name some areas. Sometimes these bodies want information to help in their decisions. Depending on the law governing the body, the strength of their request for information varies.

Negligence

The worst possible scenario for any health professional is to encounter the court system because of an accusation of doing something wrong. It is your income, assets, career and reputation on the line. Unfortunately, I had more formal training in negligence by becoming a diving instructor, than I ever did in my psychology training. In the diving industry you are trained on what constitutes negligence and how to avoid it. The situation in other professions varies widely. My contact with the medical profession has shown that there is a comprehensive focus on risk management but other areas of allied health appear to get varying but often inadequate amounts of training on these issues.

I read recently that Sydney is now second only to California in litigation. Australians like to litigate. Consequently, as practitioners, we need to understand what constitutes negligence and what type of actions are going to get us sued. The first step to understanding negligence is to understand the concept that is called in American literature the 'reasonably prudent person' (RPP) or referred to in Australian law training as the 'reasonable man or woman'. As a teaching tool, the former provides a clearer concept although the meaning is essentially the same. In the case of a psychologist, this is a fictitious ideal psychologist who always uses due care and always acts prudently in any and every circumstance. This composite of best practice is what a psychologist will be judged against. The same applies to counsellors, social workers, doctors, or any other mental health professional.

One definition of negligence is "an unintentional fault, or carelessness resulting in injury. It deals with avoidable incidents which should have been anticipated and prevented by taking reasonable precautions" (Cohen, 1995).

In the treatment literature there are 'best practice' models. These are all very interesting in theory but most of us use personalised variations of the main techniques. Many mainstream treatments such as hypnosis, acupuncture and chiropractic treatment were controversial for decades before acceptance. Had I used hypnosis 20 years ago, I would have been a minority voice within the profession. It is only because of a handful of dedicated practitioners that hypnosis survived as a psychological treatment. Creativity in the face of the professional majority would open someone up to litigation but it is also a necessary part of the development of any profession to have pioneers of new techniques who shun the conventional techniques of the day.

As many professions cannot agree on the treatment techniques, how then will the RPP be judged? The answer is that most professions agree on how the practitioners should conduct themselves. These are called ethical standards. Whether or not someone is a member of the professional organisation, they are likely to be judged against its standards. For example, if a psychologist was called into court to answer a negligence case, they would be judged against the APS Code of Ethics. Whether or not you think that the guidelines in the Code of Ethics are wrong or inappropriate, it is the majority standard. I would argue that the RPP would be aware of the Code of Ethics of their profession.

In practical terms, the following example highlights how negligence may apply. A private therapist works in a hospital. He is a bit of a joker and likes to clown around. He has a student on placement. One day he picks up a somewhat heavy briefcase and tosses it at the student. It hits her in the stomach when she failed to catch it. Later he finds out she had her appendix removed the week before and after being hit by the case, had re-opened some stitches which caused her to bleed internally. She was fine immediately after the hit but then developed complications when the wound became infected. She had two weeks in hospital with complications and had to repeat a year of the course. Was the therapist negligent?

The outcome is obviously disproportionate to the act. He did not know that she had the operation or stitches and he did not know it was going to put her in hospital for two weeks, but under negligence he did not have to actually foresee the exact consequences, only that tossing a heavy bag could cause a problem. The fact that the outcome was bigger than expected does not matter. It is not the outcome he will be found negligent upon (although the outcome will determine the size of the damages), it is the foreseeable consequences of the act. So in a case like this, the therapist may be held negligent for that injury. Negligence is not simply the act or the outcome; it is also the circumstances which have led to the outcome.

To consider negligence in more detail, it is important to consider the four main components of negligence (Cohen, 1995). These are:

1. A Duty of Care
2. A Breach of Duty
3. Causation and Proximate Cause
4. Damages

A Duty of Care

Anyone providing a professional service has a duty to provide reasonable care. As a helping professional this is implicit in every situation. So if you work with people with medical conditions, should you have CPR training? Would the RPP? If you do a lot of medical work such as in health psychology, I would argue that the reasonably prudent health psychologist, dealing with a lot of medical conditions, probably should be trained in CPR. However, if you deal with people in other areas of the profession, then there may be valid arguments why you need not be trained in first aid. You need to anticipate what a RPP would do in any given case.

Any professional has a certain degree of legal responsibility for the welfare and safety of others when they provide treatment. One of the best sources of information for those involved in counselling is the book *Risky Practices* by Michael Tunnecliffe and Nigel McBride (see reference list). It outlines many aspects which need to be understood to minimise risk.

Many professionals do not understand the breadth of the duty of care principle. An example runs along the following lines. You are running a training course and during the coffee break someone comes up and asks for a bit of clinical advice. You give them the advice, they act on it and it fails; the next minute you have a law suit. Many professionals are surprised to learn that just because they did not get paid, it does not mean that they did not have a duty of care. What Tunnecliffe and McBride argue is that in certain circumstances you have a duty of care outside the obvious patient-practitioner relationship. The bottom line is that if you give advice as a health professional, there are certain responsibilities connected to that advice which you may be held accountable for under certain circumstances.

Breach of Duty

A breach of duty is an act or failure to act that creates an unreasonable risk of harm. Suppose we choose to provide a treatment such as Aversive Conditioning for sexual addiction or administer Eye Movement Desensitisation and Reprocessing (EMDR) for treatment of trauma associated with a recent heart attack. In both cases the person has a heart attack and dies. If you were using aversive conditioning for sexual thoughts, you might be able to argue that the heart attack was not a breach of duty of care. As someone who has been trained in EMDR, you would have been told a physical abreaction is possible during treatment, then the situation could be different. If you were treating someone for the trauma associated with heart attack memories, it is not an unreasonable possibility that they could have another heart attack due to the physical abreaction. As the RPP should have been able to foresee the risks, then a court may determine that a breach of duty has taken place.

Causation and Proximate Cause

Causation and proximate cause is about explaining how the damage occurred. It is the building block in determining blame for damage. This is where the law gets technical. It is where there are complex arguments in court about the percentage that one act is responsible for causing an outcome. The heart of negligence is about whether the injury resulted from an unreasonable risk of harm that was a reasonably foreseeable consequence of the health professional's conduct.

Using the earlier example, if your client has a heart attack because of EMDR, and you know that EMDR causes abreactions, it was a reasonably foreseeable consequence. If you are using aversive conditioning to treat a 30 year old for inappropriate sexual thoughts, it may be unreasonable to have expected them to have had a heart attack. Many areas are shades of grey. For example, what about using techniques like hypnosis to recover lost memories? Take an example where the client finds memories which they believe to be true and then leaves their job and family. Later they see a special on television which questions the validity of the technique and take you to court. The lawyers will then have psychologists and psychiatrists arguing whether false memories exist or not, and arguing about the implication of particular techniques. As these professions have not resolved the debate, a court of law will make a finding on the particular point. The loser may end up with the legal costs, including the costs of various expert witnesses for both sides of the argument.

It is not the purpose of this book to highlight all the risk management areas. Interplaying on the above examples are issues of informed consent, risk to self or others, and other legal issues. If the discussion has generated questions for you, seek further advice.

Damages

For negligence to be claimed, a legally recognisable injury or loss must be shown to have occurred. If so determined, then that victim can be compensated at your expense. The non-medical areas of the health profession have historically been relatively safe from negligence claims because they tend not to cause physical harm. Failure to make someone better is not necessarily considered negligence. It may be incompetence which results in Registration Board complaints but as there was no actual damage, it is hard to sue. Typically, psychologists and counsellors do not get sued much for this reason. Because of the problems associated with medication, psychiatrists are more frequently subject to negligence claims than psychologists. However, compared to other medical specialists, psychiatrists are at the lesser end of the claim range. Areas such as obstetrics is one of the worst for claims as there are greater risks and the early age of the victim means compensation is calculated over life-time losses.

One of the areas of damage which Tunnecliffe and McBride believe has significant implications for counsellors, therapists and other mental health workers is that of financial loss. Consider this simple example. Suppose you are a counsellor teaching someone assertiveness training on an individual basis. While assertiveness is a relatively simple skill, some clients go to the other extreme when they first start practising the skill. They start telling everyone 'where to go' which is aggressive, not assertive, behaviour. They go to work and tell their boss to get stuffed and consequently they get the sack. They are unemployed for over three months and they gradually become depressed to the point where they need hospitalisation. Now they are suing you for their loss of income for three months and hospital treatment because you should have foreseen that learning assertiveness skills would have caused them to be aggressive with their boss. As you failed to adequately warn and advise against this course of action you may be found to be negligent. While I do not know whether we have had such cases within the mental health professions, the possibility is not that far-fetched.

Risk Management

Having raised issues about negligence, I would expect that you are now nervous about the implications for you as a professional. There are a handful of options open to a mental health professional. These include avoiding the risk, accepting the risk, reducing the risk and transferring the risk. This section offers an introduction to some of these issues but I would again recommend the interested reader to review *Risky Practices* by Tunnecliffe and McBride and other literature related to risk management within your specific profession.

Avoid the Risk

The first approach to risk management is simply to not do certain types of work. If you are extremely concerned about risk management, you can always quit being a professional, not talk to anyone, nor even leave your home. An extreme view, but probably the only way to avoid most risks.

A more useful and effective approach is to recognise that there are some areas of practice which can result in greater risk. For example, if you work in the family court area, expect to get Registration Board complaints and hostile responses. A Family Court lawyer recently said to me that if you have not had at least three complaints to the legal practitioners association, you are either new or not doing your job. This is because family breakdown is an emotive business and some people are unreasonable. Recognising the higher risk areas, you then choose not to work in these areas.

Accept the Risk

A second approach is to accept the risk. This involves an analysis of the benefits and the problems of particular types of work and making an informed choice. I would suspect most professionals do the work because it is available to them rather than making a choice to do certain types of work. The more you understand the risks associated with your area of work, the greater the likelihood you will manage them.

In accepting the risk, it is important to realise that it is not just about what you do. Even if you are the best in your profession, you do not have to have done something wrong for someone to take a law suit against you. An aggrieved party only has to think you have done something wrong. Even if there is a substantial trial and you are not found responsible for the damages, it may still cost you between $10,000 and $50,000 worth of legal fees to defend yourself. Lawyers are increasingly taking action using a shotgun approach. For example, you ran the assertiveness training referred to in a previous vignette, based on a theoretical model. The lawyers sue the people who wrote the model, they sue you as the person who implemented it, and then they sue the agency who employed you while you are implementing it. All three parties become part of the law suit. The lawyers then sort out who was actually responsible. You may have to have a lawyer represent you for the next two to ten years before you are found not to be a part of the problem. This may not be fair, but as noted in the introductory sections, law is not about fairness but applying rules to a dispute.

Reduce the Risk

Keeping up with current knowledge and training is an important aspect of reducing risk. When the Australian Psychological Society introduced Professional Development points (PD points) I thought it was an unnecessary burden. However, one advantage of having a PD point record is that if you went to court and a lawyer states, "you were not up-to-date with the training were you?" you can then reply: "I have met the requirements of my professional society in Professional Development training; here is my certificate to prove it".

Risk can be reduced by knowing the latest legislation and other changes. The area where legislation seems to change the most is probably workers' compensation. If you work in workers' compensation you have to find out what the current situation is or you may be providing incorrect information to your client.

Privacy legislation is another area where the health professional may get caught out. If you work for a government department, freedom of information was a concept which came out about ten years ago so public service employees are used to being accountable (see the Federal *Freedom of Information Act 1982*). In the private sector, privacy legislation has recently been introduced. It has had a huge implication for how practitioners run their activities. Unfortunately, most do not really understand the implications of it. I will cite a simple example. I was told that one of the first successful cases which used the National Privacy Principles against a health professional involved someone seeing a client for a few sessions. The patient did not pay, so the therapist sent the account to a debt collection agency. The debt collection agency contacted the patient and the person went to the Privacy Board. The Act notes that their name and address is confidential information, therefore the health professional was guilty of a breach. If you do not have a clause in your intake information which allows you to release information for debt collection, then you run the risk of breaching the Act.

Good judgment based on a reasonable assessment of the situation, is the best way to reduce risk. However, good judgment is a difficult construct to learn or indeed teach. If you act conservatively, you will tend to make good judgments.

There is some American literature which examines the frequency of being sued by qualification. The study compared degree-level, with master's degree and doctoral-level psychologists. The main finding was that the more qualified they were, the less likely they were to be sued. Such findings are likely to be replicated in other professional areas. Making sure you are properly trained, working within your area of expertise and using good judgment in all that you do, are the key ingredients to lowering risk.

Supervision, referral and peer review are processes which can help lower risk. It is important to document the fact you talked over case details with your colleagues (under the National Privacy Principles you would want to ensure the client has given consent for case discussion). A simple example is that if you are dealing with a suicidal patient, document the steps you have taken to address the risk. I have several friends who are psychiatrists. I might ring one of them up and say: "I have this person who is really suicidal. I have done the following. What do you reckon?" They reply, "oh, that's fine". I then write in my notes: 'consultation with psychiatrist Joe Bloggs, date, and note that the psychiatrist agrees with plan'. A five-minute telephone call was all it took but if I was ever in a situation where I was getting sued, I have improved my position by having psychiatric input. If it went to court, a clinical psychologist is in part seen as a suitable professional for dealing with someone who is suicidal but unless the medical issues are covered by a medical practitioner, the position may not be fully defensible. A GP is seen as a generalist who is capable of dealing with minor mental health issues but discussion with a psychiatrist would strengthen their position in a similar manner. Depending on your own profession and expertise, it is important that you do likewise. As I have been stressing, document the processes in the file.

When asked about how much detail to include in case notes, there are two opposing forces. If you are going to be sued for negligence, the more detail you have the harder it is for someone to sue you. If you write 'Referred to GP' in your notes or in your diary on the day you saw a suicidal client, then that information backs up your position – it has the appearance of truth thereby making your arguments seem more plausible. If not, in court you have to say, "I think I told them that they should talk to their doctor". The lawyer, with an incredulous tone, will bite back with "think? You said think? Do you not know for sure? How certain are you?" Hesitantly you respond, "90 per cent certain". They then put to you: "So, there's a 10 per cent chance you killed this person!" From someone who inadvertently overlooks writing a comment on a file, you become labelled responsible for killing the client. On the other hand, if someone subpoenas your file for another purpose, such as for the Family Court, the less detail included, the harder it is for them to cross-examine you.

The timing of recording case notes is also important. The closer in time the entry is recorded in your notes to when an event occurred, the more weight that will put on the information. If you write notes while talking to the person, your records would be viewed more positively than if you simply write a summary afterwards. This would still be granted more weight than a summary written at the end of the day or week. If I am writing a forensic assessment I will take verbatim notes as much as possible. I will also write down my questions and any observed behaviours at the time.

To get around this problem, some therapists tape their notes. Taped notes would probably carry more weight but you have got to weigh up whether (a) it is worth stockpiling thousands of tapes in your cupboard, and (b) whether you can afford the expense of getting them transcribed. It is a personal choice at this stage, as it is not yet an expected practice. However, after a recent Family Court case where a particular QC was very nasty to me about the note situation, I am weighing up whether I should tape my interviews or not. Similar issues apply about videotaping interviews with children. If you are interviewing children for sexual abuse investigations you will find different rules in different States. In my opinion a video serves a double purpose: firstly it records information but secondly it prevents the child from being interviewed on repeated occasions.

I was asked recently as to whether the verbatim notes scrawled out during an interview could be summarised and the original scruffy disjointed notes of the session then destroyed. From a court perspective, the verbatim notes would be considered the evidence with the most weight. From the perspective of a health professional, we do not really care about the evidence, we care about the formulation. Unfortunately, lawyers care about the evidence upon which a formulation is created. If you write notes and destroy them, be prepared to justify your procedure, and be prepared for vicious treatment in court. I am also advised that there are potentially serious legal implications for destroying evidence.

There are other ways of reducing risk. One of the things I do is I provide my clients with written or verbal agreements about what to expect. It is all about informed consent. By law, the Family Court may order a client to attend. However, I still take the time to explain confidentiality and the fact that everything a client tells me may end up in a report. I also have a letter sent to all new treatment referrals. This is sent complete with a copy of the Privacy Principles I have developed for my practice. Examples of these materials can be found in the book *Risky Practices*.

Transfer the Risk

Assuming that you continue to work as a mental health professional, what do you do about the risk? The idea of insurance is to transfer the larger share of risk from you onto somebody else. There are sometimes limits to what insurance will cover so you need to read your policy carefully. However, if you have a policy and you are successfully sued, the money does not come from your assets. If you do not have insurance they can then take the money off you by selling your house, your car, or whatever else it takes to pay the money.

The downside is that insurance costs money. In a recent newspaper (*West Australian*, 14 June, 2003) it notes that a non-procedural GP pays $7200 for their annual insurance; neurosurgeons pay $45,500; while the fee for medical obstetrics is $97,000. Psychologists complain because our insurance is now costing nearly $700 per year!

When considering the insurance coverage, most policies are Date of Claim policies. That means if you see a client in the year 2000, and the patient argues that you did something negligent but they do not file a claim until March 2005, it is the current policy for 2005 which covers you, not the 2000 policy. If you were to retire, it is important to ensure that you have sufficient coverage into the future. Roll-on cover is generally included when someone retires but what happens if someone goes from private practice back to paid employment?

There are financial strategies which can be used to minimise risk. Some accountants now advise the transfer of assets into their partner's name because it is not the couple who is sued but the individual. If you have got a partner who is not likely to be sued, and is likely to be with you in the future, there may be advantages to the assets being in their name. Seek appropriate financial advice about this type of strategy.

One of my colleagues raised an interesting consequence of having insurance and settling out of court. Years ago they had a client raise a negligence claim against them. They settled out of court for a small settlement. Since that time the practitioner has not been able to get any insurance. Settling at one point has excluded any other insurer from taking them on. The lesson here is to be very careful about what you agree to when dealing with insurance companies.

2

WRITING REPORTS FOR COURT

After receiving the lawyer's request, your information has to be put together in a manner which is useful for the court. The normal format is to write a report but sometimes your evidence may be given verbally. For reasons which will become evident later, the written report is the format which is generally required. Depending on the initial brief the report may be sent directly to the court, sworn as an affidavit, or sent to the briefing lawyer. The briefing lawyer will advise you about what they require.

Anyone who has studied human behaviour knows that presentation is everything. How you structure your report, the words used to describe things and the order in which information is presented all impact on how the report will be perceived. It is critical that you think about the structure of your report. The following sections outline some of the key principles in writing a report.

Key Principles in Report Writing

KISS Principle

Kiss means 'Keep It Simple, Stupid'. Very early in my career a barrister friend said "write your reports like the lawyers and judges are ignorant of the topic because they probably are". This is an extreme way of putting it but I accept her underlying message. When you write your report, unless they are specialist lawyers who work in the medico-legal field and are very familiar with the literature, they will not understand any but the simplest of the profession's terms. I avoid using jargon as much as possible and the safest assumption is that the reader has no previous knowledge of the area of expertise.

Consider the following example. What is domestic violence? Is it slapping your partner in the face during a fight? Is it burning your partner's clothes if you disagree? Is it smashing every piece of furniture with a baseball bat? Is it taking your partner to the bush at gunpoint and raping her? The argument is that all of these scenarios could be defined as domestic violence. The critical question is how would it help a judge in the family court if you said that domestic violence existed in this relationship? The alternative is to say the following: "This person has a set of rigid beliefs which he enforces in a demeaning way"; "This person has a temper problem which results in sudden violence"; or "This person is likely to act out, stalk and then become violent when rejected". By using a description of the behaviour, rather than simply using jargon like 'domestic violence', the court is in a much better position to make a finding.

At the other end of the scale, I sometimes run into some problems where I have kept the language too simple. I have had massive arguments about the definition of 'flighty' and 'feral children' in court reports. The terms described the situations perfectly, but I ended up with debates as to what I actually meant because the words were too colloquial.

It is important to be careful about how emotive you get. In one of my reports I used the description "worst case of psychological abuse I have seen for some time". I spent ages with a QC hammering me at the trial about the basis of the definition. While I still believe it was a worst case, the judge decided that I had been emotive in my response and felt that I had not liked the client. Much of my evidence was then discarded. The safest path is to understated rather than over-emphasising the point, i.e. avoid the emotive or the extreme.

I try to keep the language common and err towards being simplistic. There have been numerous occasions where I have had members of the legal profession consult with me to explain aspects of other professional's medical or psychological reports because they did not understand what had been written. Having read those reports myself, I can understand the lawyers' frustrations as I too had trouble following the reports. In therapy terms, if you are talking to different people, and lawyers are different people, talk in the narrative they can understand.

It is important, however, that you do not become so vague that you lose all meaning. You need to be as precise as possible and one of the worst complaints about some allied health professionals' reports is that they tend to cover too many bases. They say, "if this, then that, maybe this" and so on. Medically trained specialists such as psychiatrists will come in and say "this is the way it is" which is easier for the court. The court likes us to have an opinion, but we have got to be careful to get a balance between conservatively covering options, and not having an opinion. It is critical that you make sure you have a view but also that you show the logic leading to that view.

Citing Literature

There is an argument among certain psychologists as to whether to cite literature or not in a court report. In Western Australia this argument became quite heated because there was one psychologist who would often send in reports with up to 60 references. That person would then argue that everyone else was doing it wrong and only their approach was correct. I would argue that judges do not get any value from lists of names, nor would they seek out the literature to read the psychological references, so there seems to be no real point in including them. In other words, do not cite references unless you use them for good reason.

I was once in a trial situation before a judge where a psychologist had given a second opinion on my report criticising among other things, the lack of referencing. I was giving evidence, so I took the opportunity to seek from the judge an opinion whether or not to cite references. When I was asked a question about the literature I commented along the lines of the following: "It would be helpful to the profession if we had some guidance as to how much referencing to the professional literature we should include in our report". In his summing up, Judge Barlow stated:

> Because of the nature of psychology, more likely than not there will forever be debates and disagreements between psychologists in relation to human behaviour. Generally I do not think a court is the appropriate forum for that debate. There may be cases where a witness who purports to be an expert puts forward a view or opinion based on a theory or methodology, but is yet to gain general acceptance, or alternatively a theory or model which is yet to be completely discredited. Obviously, in such a case it would be appropriate for the court to hear evidence relevant to the credibility of the theory or methodology. However, in cases which do not fall in that category it is unlikely that detailed referencing to the psychological studies will be of any, or at least of any significant, assistance to a trial judge.

From this judgment I would argue that you only need to cite significant or controversial references and, if you are quoting from test manuals, cite that information.

However, the new guidelines for expert evidence in the Family Court of Australia state that an expert must explain the reasons for their decision. Rule 15.63 of the *Family Law Rules* notes: "An expert's report must include the following in support of the expert witness's conclusions...the literature or other material used in making the report" (as of April 2004). This requirement extends to the need for a well-considered rationale, based on the professional literature. Hence, many professionals may have to go back to the library and make sure they are well-versed on the material upon which they are basing their decisions.

I would argue that if you are offering an expert opinion, you should integrate a wide body of knowledge and not be reliant on discrete journal articles. It is critical to realise the difference between citing literature and knowing the literature. An effective expert is familiar with a wide cross-section of the literature and will be able to give examples of landmark studies if necessary. The point made here is that you do not have to cite all the articles you have ever read when preparing a report, but you must report any specific material used in writing a particular report.

A side issue with referencing is the practice that I have seen in Western Australia where some of my colleagues will use computer interpretations of psychological tests like the Millon Inventories or Wechsler computer scoring systems and include verbatim chunks in their reports. I would never use computer-generated interpretation in court because it is not my opinion but a computer's opinion. I would always score the protocol and offer my opinion of what the test means in my own words. In the medical sector, it is the difference between relying on a radiologist's report of a scan or personally looking at the scan results and offering an opinion. The first is another's expertise; the second is relying on their own expertise. Everyone can look at the raw data, but the expert has the experience and knowledge to offer an opinion about what the data actually means. Therefore, it is critical to reference sources of the material which is not of your own opinion.

Ultimate Issue

During a trial, the judge sits in court listening to lawyers asking questions of witnesses as they drone on for hours. The judge does not have to do much other than make comments about the odd principle of law, guide the process, and to stay awake while they gather information upon which to base their findings. At the end of all the evidence, the judge's (if there is not a jury) one bit of excitement is to hand down a finding. The judge has formed a view about all the information and gets the chance to say, "guilty for these reasons", "not guilty", or "I will make this decision or recommend this much compensation". This fundamental decision is called the ultimate issue. It is the prerogative of the judge alone to make the ultimate judgment.

Understanding the concept of ultimate issue is critical as it draws the line between where health workers should finish their arguments and where the judge's exclusive role begins. The most common mistake made by people inexperienced with the court is that they overstep the mark and try to take over the judge's role. For example, when it comes time for the trial, if I am asked a question like, "where do you think the children should live in this family court matter?" I would respond: "I provided my opinions to the court in a report based on the evidence I had. At this time the trial has been going for three days, the judge has information available to him or her which I am not privy too, therefore residence is now their decision and my views no longer matter." Usually the judge starts nodding in agreement and says to the lawyer, "yes, Dr Watts is right" which quickly stops the lawyer from asking that line of questioning. It is respectful to the court to let the judge have his or her role. Even if asked to explain further, this approach shows respect to the judge. They do not want some social worker coming in and saying where the children should live, an accountant saying how the property should be divided, nor a psychologist saying whether the felon is guilty!

The approach to take when you write your report is to lead the judge to make a logical conclusion from your report. If you are writing a pre-sentence report, you do not say how long the sentence should be or whether it should be in prison or not. However, you can outline the factors which indicate whether this person should get a custodial sentence such as suicide risk in custody, institutionalisation, vulnerability, impact on rehabilitation, risk to the community, and so on. For example, I wrote in a report: "This man is from the Kimberley Region of Western Australia. He has never been outside of that region. The charges he is involved in are serious but bringing him to Perth will be harder on him than it would be on a person who normally lives in Perth. I understand the court has various considerations to make in such a case, but in terms of this man's psychological needs, the sooner he can be returned to his community the better he will cope." I have not told the judge what to do but hopefully I have shown him or her a logical possibility.

In 2002, I contacted the Chief Judge of the Western Australian District Court to see if he could offer a brief comment on what constitutes good evidence from psychological witnesses. Judge Hammond kindly asked Judge Wisbey to prepare a paper (with permission of the judge, I have reproduced the paper in its entirety in the appendices). Judge

Wisbey had this to say about the ultimate issue:

> A psychologist in a personal injury case or a criminal proceeding can give evidence that he or she carried out an examination or testing of a person, and that the testing did or did not reveal any abnormality in the person tested. He or she cannot express an opinion that the tested person is genuine or malingering. The opinion must not extend to usurping the function of the trial judge in reaching the ultimate conclusion as to whether the person is truthful. That opinion is not admissible as the court is well able and required to draw the appropriate conclusion from the evidence presented.

If you are going to address the question of malingering, it is important that you outline the facts where the assessment was consistent with someone who maybe malingering, but you are better off not to state that "this person is malingering". You should state something along the lines of the following: "On the test of Memory Malingering, they failed extremely badly when even a person with a substantial head injury can complete this test to an adequate degree, therefore it shows major inconsistencies in their evidence. On the Millon Personality Test they had an extremely high Desirability scale, which also suggests they were presenting in a very favourable light, therefore the evidence is highly questionable." Then the judge can say, "On the strength of all the evidence, this person is malingering".

Another way to conceptualise your role in court is to link the ultimate issue to your evidence base. An expression which I find useful is 'from a psychological perspective'. The advantage of this term is that you are telling the court you are only one part of the evidence picture. It is about acknowledging the limitations of the evidence. You are a psychologist giving psychological evidence and you do not have all the facts. Never assume you ever will have all the facts. The same principle applies to medical doctors or social workers. You are offering the court your perspective; it is now up to the judge to apply it to the legal perspective.

This discussion on ultimate issue may seem like splitting hairs but the subtlety is critical. Following the principle is a demonstration of both respect to the court and acknowledging the limits of your evidence. I found it much less stressful when I realised the court made the decisions; I only serve to assist the court.

Confidentiality

Many practitioners provide treatment on the assumption that the confidentiality they value with their clients is protected in the legal arena. Unfortunately, this is generally not the case. The Australian Psychological Society's Ethical Guidelines state: "No privilege in Common Law protects communications between a psychologist and a client and because courts can scrutinise documents and files, all consultations and discussions should be recorded". My enquiries suggest that this also applies to all other professions – even medical doctors have difficulty claiming confidentiality of their information.

Law works on the assumption that evidence can be collected and used in court. Once in court, some professionals think that writing 'confidential' will protect their reports from public discussion. This is just not the case. When you write something, all the lawyers involved need copies of the reports so they can prepare their cases. I work on the assumption that any report sent to the court will be handed around like birthday cake at a children's party. Everyone gets some. In court the parties likely to see the report include the judge, the lawyers for both sides, the individuals involved, and all other incidental participants in the process. You need to write your report knowing that your client will read it and that other people will read it as well.

Sometimes you may be unlucky enough to be involved in a case where there are really nasty dynamics with potentially fatal consequences. For example, I was involved in a case where a man had a history of violence, a current major depression, perceived his children as property, had recently separated from his wife, and had suicidal ideation involving himself and homicidal ideation involving the children. This was the profile of a man who could drive to the bush then gas himself and children. I wrote the required report but I ensured I received advice about how to manage the process by telephoning the judge's associate at the court. I was told to provide a covering letter to the report and include the comment: "In my opinion this person is high risk. I recommend this report should not be released until some safeguards are put in place". While it was an unusual step, the court did not release the report until the day of the hearing so as to protect the children.

In another Family Court case, a colleague of mine assessed a particular father as someone who was highly dangerous. There were strong indicators that he was a life-long psychopath. The psychologist explained the situation to the children's lawyer and he was advised not to write a report but provide his evidence verbally so that there was an element of surprise. This was allowed by the court. While these are exceptional circumstances it is helpful to know that there are options for dealing with difficult situations. To find out the options for minimising risks, either talk to the legal officers involved or to other professionals experienced in the area.

Another interesting point to note is that in the Australian Psychological Society Ethical Guidelines it states: "If confidential information must be disclosed in court, and the client is not party to the legal proceedings, the client should be advised by the psychologist of the time and date of the trial". What this means is if a psychologist sees a couple for family therapy before they separated, and then one of them then comes up before a court on a workers' compensation matter, this issue may arise. For example, if the lawyer subpoenas your file and asks you to attend court, you are obliged to notify the other party of the time and place you are going to give evidence. You have a professional obligation to notify them. I am uncertain as to whether this is part of the ethical guidelines of other professions but at a minimum it does represent professional courtesy. The amount of disclosure becomes difficult as you balance the requirements for confidentiality as contained in the Code of Ethics and National Privacy Principles on one hand and the legal requirements of disclosure on the other hand.

The issues are simplified by the use of what is called informed consent. It is important that before you treat someone they know what you are doing. The use of a consent letter allows the client to understand the strengths and limitations of what you are doing. They can choose to participate or not.

The same applies to the release of information. Having a person sign a release of privacy information helps to set up a paper trail so that if there are repercussions, you can defend yourself. If a lawyer requests a report, it is good practice to ensure the client signs a release so that information can be sent. Often the lawyer will provide a signed release. If not, ensure that you get one. The only exceptions are in cases where an Act compels the release of information, such as a court expert in the Family Court, where there are mandatory reporting requirements of abuse, or with certain aspects of the workers' compensation system, e.g. funding based on a requirement to provide regular treatment reports. This is where knowledge of local law is critical. Even if the person has come for a report, they may not understand how that report is going to be used, who it will be released to, or how they can get a copy.

Similarly, when I first started doing Family Court assessments, my office received a lot of phone calls from people complaining that they did not know what was going on after the report was released. A particularly effective way of managing this situation has been the inclusion of 'notes to the parties' at the beginning or end of the report. For example, in the family court I include the new rules which outline the process for asking a question of an expert, after offering some general directions. The following represents my current statement:

> If you have any concerns with the report, discuss them with your legal representative. If you do not have your own lawyer, either seek independent legal advice or write to the Separate Representative outlining your concerns.
>
> Please do not make telephone contact with me or my office after the report has been released. Any communication must be in writing (as outlined below), otherwise my position of independence may be jeopardised.
>
> Under Rule 15.65 of the Family Law Rules (2004) it states that you may ask questions about an expert's report. However:
>
> Questions must be in writing and can only be put once.
>
> I.   It must be within 21 days from when you received the report.
>
> II. Questions can only be for the purpose of clarifying the report.
>
> III. The questions must not be vexatious or oppressive, or require the expert to undertake an unreasonable amount of work.
>
> IV. You must give a copy of any questions to each other party.
>
> V.   A single expert witness's reasonable fees and expenses incurred in answering any questions are to be paid by the party ASKING the questions (my rates are based on the APS schedule of fees).
>
> A single expert witness is not required to answer any questions until the fees and expenses for answering them are paid or secured.

This does not stop the impulsive, brain-damaged, drug-using client from ringing up, but the more intelligent ones will read it and then use the appropriate channels because they now know what is expected of them.

Credibility

To be successful in court, it is important to manage the credibility of your evidence. The first point is to make sure that you are knowledgeable and correct.

One psychological example involved a criminal case where a boy was aged about 13 years but had a low IQ. Under the Western Australian law, it had to be proved that a young person knew they ought not to commit the offence before they could be convicted. The legal argument centred on the child's level of understanding. I assessed this boy using the Wechsler Intelligence Scale for Children (WISC-III). I then combined my test results and clinical impression to estimate his functional IQ being of an average nine and a half year old. My report was sent to another psychologist who also assessed the boy. This psychologist wrote a critique of my report. He advised his briefing lawyer that "Dr Watts is wrong. You cannot calculate an age-equivalent score from the Wechsler, you can only do it from the Stanford-Binet".

I went to my test manual and copied the table where it is possible to calculate age-equivalent levels using the subtests. I calculated all the age-equivalent scores, added them all up, took the average, and fortunately the score worked out to be 9.6 years. I was pretty well spot on with my estimate. When the matter went to trial, the police prosecutions lawyer launched in with the question: "You can't calculate mental age equivalence with the Wechsler can you?" I responded with "yes, I can" but he was so sure of himself that he was halfway through the next question before he realised what I had said. He stopped in his tracks and I then explained my views and handed out a copy of the table from the manual. The net result was a favourable judgment for me, while the other psychologist was criticised by the judge.

My knowledge did several things. Firstly, it made me look good in court and at the end of the day I was seen as the more credible expert. Secondly, it made the other psychologist look incompetent for not knowing the manual. Finally, it took the wind out of the prosecutor's sails and from then on he was tentative with his questions because I was apparently more knowledgeable than he was and he did not want any more surprises.

An important aspect of credibility is to remember that the judges have usually been around for years. They start out as lawyers and then become barristers. They may become Queen's Counsels and then finally they are asked to be judges. By this time they have been around for many years. This may be your first professional report for any particular court, but the judge has been reading reports for years. As a simple example, I have done nearly 300 Family Court reports as a court appointed expert. There are only about a dozen Family Court judges and magistrates in the WA court so that means each of them may have read an average of twenty-five of my reports.

Law loves the use of precedent. Precedent means that a decision made on the basis of one case will become the standard in the next case until it is challenged at a higher level. From a witness's perspective, it is important to be very careful with what you do in each situation as it may become the precedent in another situation. Without a bit of foresight, it can come back to haunt you. For example, when I was studying at university I did a psychology major and a minor degree in indigenous Australian anthropology. I then worked in the juvenile justice area where I had to assess a number of indigenous individuals in a variety of contexts. Recently, I was requested to be a court expert in a case where a white mother was murdered by the indigenous father. It was a custody dispute between the indigenous and caucasian grandparents of the children who had lost a mother and had a father in prison. I was to be appointed as the court expert but there was a clause included that there was to be a cultural adviser appointed to advise me of indigenous issues. When I found out about that clause, I refused to do the assessment. If I had done the assessment with a cultural adviser, any time I gave evidence in any court on indigenous issues it could be then used against me. The lawyer could say: "You needed a cultural adviser in that particular case in the Family Court; surely that means you are not qualified to provide opinions about indigenous people in this court?"

I refused to work with the adviser, not because I did not think they would be beneficial, but because I did not want to get locked into a precedent where I needed assistance to assess indigenous clients. The irony in this case was that it was the family law section of the Aboriginal Legal Services of Western Australia who were arguing that I needed a cultural adviser, an organisation for which at the time I was completing one or two pre-sentence reports a month for their criminal law section. I believe the lawyer was just playing a legal game to help her client, but had I fallen for the trap, and it could have had a tremendous impact on my future ability to give evidence in court.

A point to always remember is that you are only as good as your last report. Years ago, one of my colleagues wrote in a juvenile offender presentence report to the Children's Court President: "This young man shows no characteristics of a repeat sex offender and is not likely to sex offend again" but within two weeks of sentencing had committed a horrendous sex offence. This psychologist never worked again in the Children's Court. The reason why the psychologist could not work again is best highlighted in a simple experience. I gave evidence at a Family Court trial on a particularly messy case. After the case I immediately left to drive to my office which is just ten minutes away from court. The phone rang as I walked into the office and was told by a different lawyer how well I did in court that morning. The moral of the story is the legal profession is relatively small within specialist areas and the lawyers network with each other. If you do a good job, it generates lots of work. If you do a bad job, they will use that against you.

It may sound obsessive, but I keep a record of my case involvement because it helps argue credibility. To be able to say: "I have been appointed as a court expert in 300 Family Court cases" is a strong line to use. To say, "I have given evidence in lots of cases" seems to lose something. Add the statistical record to a string of credibility statements such as, "I've got a Doctor of Philosophy and a Master of Clinical Psychology. I have been working as a professional for 14 years, and I have seen 300 families in the Family Court as court expert" and it starts me in a credible position. Suppose the other party is a new graduate who has just finished a master's degree, is provisionally registered and has completed their first family court case. Who will the court put the most weight of evidence on? I will start off with a much higher credibility. The trial process may lead the court to eventually decide I am a blithering idiot, or factually did not have enough information, while the new graduate could be seen as wonderfully sensible but my experience and qualifications gives me the head start.

Even with a good qualification and experience base, lawyers will play games to challenge you credibility. One technique they can use is a line of questioning which discounts your experience. Consider the following line of questioning: "How many times have you been the court expert in the Family Court?" to which I would respond "about 300". They then follow up with, "and in how many cases have you assessed someone who is an indigenous Australian?" Being suspicious of where they are taking me I respond: "Probably about 80 of those cases". Then the crunch question of "how many cases have you assessed where an indigenous father has killed a white mother?" I then have to answer: "Well, this is my second case". In scoffing tones the lawyer then queries "and you call yourself an expert?" If I am quick I chip in "but the principles of best interest of children is not an indigenous issue but rests on general principles of developmental psychology, of which I have immense experience".

Structure of Reports

The actual process of writing a report is something which is taught at university. However, I find that the academic approach teaches how to write reports for others within the profession, or in the general health area, but not for the legal arena. This section addresses the issue of how to write a report for court. Keeping in mind the general principles already discussed, the next step is how to structure the information. There is no one perfect structure to a court report but certain elements should be included.

Date

While dating a report seems obvious, from time to time I am asked to make modifications to a report. It becomes critical to ensure that altered copies are correctly dated so that when asked to admit a report into evidence in court the corrected report is the basis of your evidence. The date is the most obvious identifying feature for reports which have been changed.

From ethical and impartiality points of view, should you change your report at the request of a lawyer? By writing a report which the lawyer wants, it ensures that you get repeat business. The cost of it is that you are no longer an impartial writer. By being a hired gun or ghost writer for the lawyer, you are doing a disservice to both court and the profession. It is critical to consider the implications carefully before changing a report once you have finished it.

For me, the critical variable in deciding whether to change a report is the nature of the change. If I am changing my opinion at the request of the lawyer, I am being unethical. It is not uncommon, however, for a lawyer to ring up and ask for a paragraph to be deleted or a sentence changed. One of the first issues to sort out would be why they want the change. If it is because you have factual errors (e.g. a date, name or place is wrong) you should change it. Similarly, typographical errors or omissions may be identified and if significant should be changed. Likewise, if you have included something which under rules of evidence is not admissible, your forensic logic will be flawed. Therefore, it may be legally appropriate to remove it. On the other hand, I would never change my opinion on the basis of a request. Ethically, an opinion should not be negotiable nor should it be for sale. If you are provided with new information which changes your opinion, it is a different matter. However, I would recommend that you do not actually change your original report but provide a supplementary or updated report which outlines the new information and explains the reason why you changed your opinion.

In cases where the request is about wording, rules of evidence, or other factors not obvious to me, then I consider it on the merit of the individual situation. Some simple examples to highlight the decision-making process are as follows. I wrote a report for a lady involved in a negligence claim after her husband was killed. I described her as 'grieving'. The solicitor wanted me to explain whether it was normal grief (which cannot be compensated) or whether the grief was pathological in some way. The request seemed reasonable so I elaborated on the issue in a supplementary report. In another case, when I was writing a pre-sentence report, I went into a lot of detail about the account of an offence as given to me by the offender. The lawyer explained that at the trial the judge made a different finding about the fact of the crime. He asked me to remove the details of the offence as now recounted. I agreed but only on the basis that I could point out that the offender's account was different. This allowed me to raise the issue I wanted to raise, but avoided problems associated with introducing another version of the crime into the court. A third example comes from a Family Court case. In an urgent report just before a trial, I made reference to information given to me by a school principal. I was told that the classroom teacher (who had a different opinion to the principal) was giving evidence at the trial but the principal was not. Therefore any evidence from the principal could not be considered by the trial judge. Hence I amended my report as I could not draw on the material for an opinion.

Some examples of requests upon which I have refused to make changes to the report included a lawyer in a Workers' Compensation case asking me to remove a paragraph where I outlined concern about the consistency of a client's information; a pre-sentence report on a dangerous offender where I was asked to remove the assessment of risk to the community; and a Family Court report where I was asked to not include the test results which showed a high elevation on Antisocial Personality Disorder on one of the parties.

In my opinion, making these types of changes would have compromised my integrity as an independent professional opinion for the court. In all cases I have done further work for the law firms so my standing for principle did not seem to damage my reputation. In fact, one lawyer later complimented me for my integrity.

One of the worst examples I had to deal with involved a case where I was asked to provide a critique of another psychologist's report. I provided this as a written report. Later, the law firm sent me an affidavit to swear where they had just summarised selected extracts of my report and wanted me to swear just the sections they were interested in but not include the entire report. Normal practice is to swear a brief affidavit stating who I am, why I did the report, and then the report in its entirety, is appended. The law firm did not want to include the entire report. I did not agree with how they had summarised some of my opinions out of context so I rewrote the section they sent me. They were not happy with my response. We ended up bartering for about a week until I could get something I was ethically happy with and the lawyer could use. This is a rare experience but unfortunately is one of the pitfalls possible.

Orientate the Reader

Writing a good report is about telling a story to the court. As with any type of story, the report has a theme, structure and purpose. I believe that all reports by health professionals are written to help explain the reason why a particular situation has come about and what the future possibilities are. Therefore, when someone picks up the report, the first section should explain why this particular report was completed. It should answer questions such as who was the referring person, and what did they want in the report. In other words, preface the story with a brief orientation.

The initial section of the report would generally explain why you believe you are appropriately qualified for this type of assessment. I provide a few sentences which summarise my experience and qualification relevant to the particular case. I then append my curriculum vitae to the report. My CV is one page of small print (font size 10) which captures various aspects of my career but especially in regards to various legal areas. I offer to provide a full ten-page resumé should they want further information. This helps the lawyer to understand whether I was suitably qualified for the type of assessment, which as you will understand later in this book, is a critical part of the cross-examination process. By addressing the issue here (at least in brief) you will spend less time in court being qualified as a witness. Unless of course you were not appropriately qualified in which case this section will highlight your flaws and allow the court to disqualify you as a witness.

Authority

If you have followed a particular code of practice when writing a report, it is useful to make a statement to that effect. For example, in New South Wales, some courts require that you make a statement that you have read Rules for Expert Practice (e.g. the District Court Rule for Expert Practice). You are then required to state that you have kept to these standards. In medico-legal areas, especially workers' compensation, there may be protocols about the type of report required, if so, state that you have written the report according to the protocols. This helps both the court and client to understand why a report was written in a particular way.

The *Family Law Rules 2004* (Rule, 15.62) which require an elaborate statement to be included in the affidavit attached to the report. Not only does the necessary authority need to be included but an awareness of the procedures, obligations and rules. As taken from the Attorney General's Department web site, the affidavit must state:

> I have made all the enquiries I believe are necessary and appropriate and to my knowledge there have not been any relevant matters omitted from this report, except as otherwise specifically stated in this report.
>
> I believe that the facts within my knowledge that have been stated in this report are true.
>
> The opinions I have expressed in this report are independent and impartial.
>
> I have read and understand Part 15.5 of the Family Law Rules 2004 and have used my best endeavours to comply with it.
>
> I have complied with the requirements of the following professional codes of conduct or protocol, being [state the name of the code or protocol].
>
> I understand my duty to the court and I have complied with it and will continue to do so.

Information Sources

To understand the basis of the evidence, the standard practice is to outline whom, when and for how long the patient was seen. It is important to list what documents you received and so forth. For reasons which will become clearer later in this book, your sources are critical for lawyers to understand the appropriateness of the evidence base. As the credibility of your report is going to be judged against the source of your information it is important to clearly list all information used in reaching your conclusions.

Privacy Issues

I am increasingly including a short paragraph which outlines privacy issues. I state how a person has consented to the release of the confidential information, that is, verbal or written consent, or a by lawyer-provided consent form. This is in case someone raises issues to do with the National Privacy Principles or places a complaint with the Registration Board. It may help me to avoid having to explain consent issues because they are spelt out in black and white in the report.

Limitations and Cautions

In my reports I will outline major limitations to the approach I took in writing the report so the lawyers can see if I am credible. I spell out the boundaries for the range of my report. A reader should know what I did and did not do. If something falls outside my area of expertise, then I state it, either in a separate section or in the body of the report. For example, if you have only seen the father in a Family Court dispute, write something like, "I have just seen the father but I understand there are two sides to every story and acknowledge I do not have the mother's version of events". Do not list every weakness in your methodology as it makes you sound incompetent. Rather, focus on the significant factors.

The court does not deem you to be an expert in everything. Only be an expert where you actually have expertise. It is the major limits you need to address. For example, in a Family Court case, I was asked to do a risk assessment where there was a case of physical abuse. I was given photographs of the abuse. I needed to make a judgment about the severity of the abuse from the photos as one factor in offering an opinion about the degree of supervision required. However, as a psychologist I have no special expertise in assessing bruising or injury patterns. That is exactly what I stated in my report.

Relevant History

I always put a summary of the history of what has led to the situation because the psycho-social dynamics are important information for any mental health professional. Avoid going over every detail of the client's life unless it has relevance. As an example, outlining every primary school attended or how they did in each grade of primary school may only be relevant in a case where neuropsychological impairment is an issue. In most cases the history should simply be summarised. The goal of writing this section is to tell the story of the person so the various items of information fit together.

Clinical Observations

One of the mental health professional's most important pieces of information is in regards to the observations about the client's presentation. Under the heading of 'Clinical Observation' I write down comments such as "this person's manner of speech was normal" or, "they seemed nervous because they kept fidgeting in the chair..." Saying that they were dressed in blue jeans and a green T-shirt and they had a nice earring is not terribly helpful unless it is leading to something else such as depression because of their unkempt appearance. The clinical observation is about outward demeanour leading to opinions of underlying diagnosis.

Test Results

Tests conducted by a health professional are just another source of information. Whether the testing is a personality test given by a psychologist, CT-scans by a radiologist, or a functional assessment by an occupational therapist, it is all important information which needs to be documented. I treat the test results as a separate source of information. I outline what tests I have used, including the version, and I briefly explain why I have used them.

Of critical importance is that I try to explain the test results in lay terms. Unless the results are user friendly for the non-professional, this section will be one of the least utilised areas of the report. For example, if I am referring to IQ scores, most non-mental health people do not understand IQ scores. However, they do understand percentiles. So I will write: "This person's IQ was in the average range, which means that out of 100 same aged people they would be in the middle 50" or "this person showed fairly significant intellectual deficits, in keeping with someone who is in the bottom one in a 100 same-aged peers in the general community." It does not take training as a psychologist to follow what I am talking about. If I am doing a report where complicated testing is needed, such as in a case where there is neuropsychological testing, I will put the technical results, including raw scores, in appendices. In the body of the report I summarise relevant tests in simple language. The appended test results keep confusing details out of the main body of the report. This allows the report to flow smoothly.

Terms of Reference and Discussion

When a lawyer writes to you, or a court order is made appointing you to undertake an assessment, they usually ask you some questions which they want addressed. These issues are called Terms of Reference. It is imperative that somewhere in your report you answer the questions item by item. If you do not answer the questions, or the answers are not easy to find in the report, then you have not done a good job. The lawyer has asked these questions for good legal reasons so try to answer them, whether you understand the relevance of the question or not.

If a lawyer approaches me and asks me to write a report on a client I am seeing for therapy, I ask them to send me a letter confirming this and to include the issues they would like me to address. If they do not specify issues, it makes it difficult to know exactly what to write in the report.

People trained in mental health approaches may be tempted to use terms like 'formulation'. Other mental health professionals may know what this means but most lawyers probably will not have any idea. Formulation is a great practice in the consulting room but in court you have opinions, not formulations. Avoid using a therapy approach to legal reports.

I often find that the terms of reference do not allow me to tell the story about how a situation came about. Therefore, I have a discussion section which allows me to raise the various issues necessary to explain what is going on. In terms of logical flow, this may come before the terms of reference but there are no hard and fast rules as to what structure gets the message across in the most logical and succinct fashion.

Conclusion

One day I was sitting in the Legal Aid Office with a lawyer when my report was delivered from the court. This 18-page document that I had carefully constructed was flipped to the last page and my conclusion read. The report was then put to one side. The moral of the story is that the last thing written in the report is often the first, and sometimes only, section which will be read. Careful crafting of the conclusion is paramount to your role. Of course there are pedantic lawyers who will read the report from cover to cover and examine every word so the whole thing needs to be thorough. I am not sure which style of lawyer is more concerning!

Appendices

Anything which interferes with the flow of the report, but may be relevant to your evidence, can be included in appendices. I include my CV, test results and other key information as appendices. These may be useful to another professional but not to the flow of the report.

3

THE RELIABLE WITNESS

As you approach the time to give evidence in court, hopefully you handled the initial lawyer's request well and structured yourself to be as independent as the circumstances would allow. You have then provided a carefully crafted report to either the briefing lawyer or court. The next step is to give evidence in court. You are now in a position to become a reliable or credible witness.

The Reliable Witness

The concept of a reliable witness is interesting in that my training as a psychologist taught me that validity was about whether a test measured what it was supposed to be measuring (did it give a true measure), while reliability was about getting the same results each time a test was administered. However, in law the terms are used in almost the opposite way. A reliable witness is not someone who turns up on time or gives the same answer each time – a reliable witness is someone who is seen as truthful to the court. They provide information which can be relied upon.

To understand the concept of a reliable witness you have to understand evidence from a lawyer's point of view. To explain I will begin with a philosophical question, and that is the question of what is truth? One of Western Australia's forensic pathologists gave an example where there was a fatal train accident at a rail crossing at an outer suburb. What happened was that a number of witnesses on a railway platform, who heard a bang, saw the boom gate coming down onto the bonnet of a car as the car came across the railway crossing only to be smashed by a passenger train. All of these witnesses said they saw the boom gate coming down on the car. In other words, their evidence was of a mechanical fault. This particular suburb has somewhat of a problem with crime so a number of security cameras were operating on the platform. One of these security cameras captured what happened at the railway crossing. The video showed that the car hit the boom gate causing the bang which the witnesses heard and forced the boom gate up. The witnesses turned and saw the gate coming down for a second time with the train hitting the car. The truth was that it was not a mechanical failure but human error on the part of the driver. The issue this example highlights is that the court was not present at the time, and rarely do they have a video of what happened, so they do not know the direct truth. The court uses witnesses to infer a version of the truth based on evidence.

For mental health workers, there is no objective reality to much of our work, only theoretical constructs. Terms such as Depression, Post-Traumatic Stress Disorder, Battered Wife Syndrome cannot be seen or measured directly. Symptoms and behaviours are observed and diagnoses are inferred. This is why different professionals often come to different judgments.

The court then sets about trying to make a finding based on reports given by witnesses. They determine findings to help infer about what is 'true'. There are different methods of doing this but the one commonly used in Australian court systems is the adversarial system. To illustrate the point using an example, if I said I had a piece of string, how do you actually know it is a piece of string unless you see it? The way the society does this is to appoint an independent person to oversee the situation (a judge) and then have two sides test the case. I would give the material to one person and they look at it and say: "That is a nice piece of string, it has got fibres twisted together, it is the colour of string, the size of string, so it must be string". I then give it to somebody else who can offer a critical assessment. They say: "No, that is not a piece of string." They pull it and try and break it, and then argue about the makeup of the fibres. At the end of it all, the judge decides whether or not it is a piece of string on what he or she was told but without ever seeing it.

The court does the same thing with your evidence. When in court someone is firstly going to go over your report to draw out the strengths. Then someone else is going to pick holes in it to prove it is not a good report. At the end of it a judge rules on how the report measured up. Lawyers call this process testing the evidence.

When you provided your report to the court it is untested. However, because you wrote it you think it is true, which is why so many health professionals find court such a taxing process. We 'know' that what we wrote is true and we believe we have done our work to the best of our abilities. Then we go into court and some lawyer tries to say we got some or all of it wrong. If you can understand that the court does not have first-hand access to the truth, only witnesses who bring material to the court, the perspective changes. It is not about you as a person. It is a testing process by people who were not there when it happened. Once the evidence has undergone the rigours of the testing process the court can put weight on it. However, if you have not done a good job setting the situation up, when they tug the string, the report falls apart. The manner of testing involves a series of steps outlined in the next section.

Process of Testing the Evidence

Swearing In

When you walk into court, the first thing which happens is you are sworn in. You either swear an oath or make an affirmation. This means you either swear on the Bible or you affirm to tell the truth.

In the old days our word used to mean something. These days when someone gives you their word, it probably lasts as long as it takes to say it. The swearing in is a custom which is considered important by the court. It is supposed to mean something and historically, even 100 years ago, people would use expressions like 'my word is my bond' and have meant it. Hopefully, you do tell the truth because you believe in that process.

Evidence-in-Chief

The first part of the testing of your evidence is the evidence-in-chief. The lawyer who has called you to give evidence generally is the person who is going to lead you through your evidence. There are several formalities which usually take place. Firstly, they get you to state your name, address and qualification. They go through the processes of qualifying you as a witness by highlighting the expertise you have and its relevance to the case. This varies from simply stating your qualification to detailed examination of skills and expertise.

Generally, you have written a report and a copy of the report is formally tended to the judge by the lawyer. This process involves you seeing a copy and stating that it is the report you wrote. If there is more than one version of your report, do make sure that the correct one was tended.

The next part of the evidence in chief is the lawyer drawing out information from you relevant to their position. Generally, they say nice things about your report, unless your report was unfavourable and they had to tender it anyway. In this case they may be quite biting in the examination of the report.

Cross-examination

After the 'friendly' lawyer has finished, the opposition's job is to represent their client's position, particularly by exposing the flaws and the weaknesses in your report. The cross-examination is the part of giving evidence that every witness dreads. This is the confrontational aspect of the adversarial approach. The cross-examining lawyer's job is to show that you do not have the truth.

If you read any law book on cross-examination, there are a range of different areas lawyers can cross-examine you on, but they generally cover five broad areas of attack. The first challenge to any witness is qualification and experience. One of the reasons I did a PhD was to look better in court – "Dr Watts" has more authority than "Mr Watts". I try not to play the qualification game but from time to time I have been forced to play it. For example, one day I had a solicitor ask: "Mr Watts, you shouldn't be able to answer that because you are not a doctor". I said: "Well, actually it's Dr Watts, and I can answer that because I am qualified in this area as a psychologist". Sometimes the game gets more subtle. I had one case where I was doing a social security overpayment criminal trial and was arguing that my client was suffering from major depression. It was put to me by a cunning lawyer: "Well you cannot prescribe, can you?" I had to say "no" and he would not let me elaborate.

Another way that a lawyer will try to show you are not adequately qualified is to break down your experience as given in the earlier example about the indigenous father who killed his white wife and the grandparents were fighting for custody of his children. These approaches are ploys and judges often see through them, but if you get shaken in the opening gambit, there is more chance the barrister will force you to crumble in your later evidence where it really matters.

If you are a new graduate not being experienced can be a problem. If all else fails, go back to your qualifications. However, this may or may not be useful. I was talking to a lawyer about a case where the witness was a Psychologist Registrar who had done a master's degree but was still in her first year of supervised practice. She was asked in a Family Court case: "Have you got any experience in the area of attachment?" She gave a really good come-back: "I haven't worked with children but I have studied it at a theoretical level in my university degree". However, the judge said: "Next line of questioning, this witness is not qualified to answer questions of attachment". He was not going to accept her expertise because she had not worked with children.

Ethically, it is important to stay within your area of expertise, whether newly qualified or very experienced. You do not have to be an expert on everything. The court will afford you greater respect if you state when you are being asked about subjects beyond your field of knowledge.

Historically, there has been a hierarchy to the weighting of the value experts. In the past the evidence from a psychiatrist outweighed a psychologist, who outweighed a social worker. A counsellor probably would not have been seen as qualified to give expert evidence. From the perspective of my profession, psychology has done a good job in clawing back the distance. I find in Western Australia that a good psychologist's report is generally equal to that of a psychiatrist's report in many courts now. A 1995 judgment in Victoria (*R v David Joel Whitbread*) noted that once the question of medical treatment was put aside, psychologists were found to be equal, and depending on knowledge and experience, possible better than some psychiatrists concerning mental states and processes of the mind. Likewise, social workers are also gaining in credibility in the court but appear to have some distance to go.

The practical reality is that there are some judges who have been around for decades and refer back to when psychiatrists were the only experts they felt were qualified to give evidence and they did not think psychologists and social workers were worth having in court. On the other hand, there are some new judges who are only too happy to hear psychological evidence. Therefore, qualification and the usefulness of an expert is not only case specific but it is judge specific. It is important to remember that good evidence is good evidence, even if you are newly qualified or from a different profession.

The second aspect the cross-examining lawyer is going to challenge is the perceived impartiality of the witness. They are going to try to show you are biased. That is where the information contained in the first half of this book comes in. If you set up your position to be as independent as possible this attack will be minimised. What they want to argue is that you are biased, subjective, work for one side, and are only saying positive things to protect your client. You have a choice. You can either argue that you offer an independent opinion or give evidence of fact.

If you are in a therapy role one way to handle it is to agree with the bias and acknowledge the limits of your position and only provide evidence of fact. "Yes, I was representing my client's position. I understand there are two sides to every story and I accept that I only have one side. However, in seeing that one side, I have observed the following..." Rather than give an opinion you give factual evidence based on observations. The alternative is to try and give opinion evidence by minimising biases.

Preventing attacks on your objectivity should be managed by the little things you did along the way. For example, when were you paid for writing the report? I try to get paid before I release the report. This is for two reasons: one you get paid because everyone wants to see the report but, more importantly, you can say, "they paid for my time, they did not pay for my opinion. I was paid before my opinion was released".

The third area of challenge is upon the factual basis of your material. This is the material you have based your evidence on. They are going to start knocking holes in the observations, test data, historical information, and interview material. If your assessment can be shown to be inadequate, then your findings might be seen as questionable. Once again, a well-structured methodology and a clearly written report is the best defence against this attack.

Unfortunately, the rules of evidence are complex and the legal profession has the upper hand in challenges to the factual basis. For example, I interviewed a 19-year-old girl whose uncle had allegedly sexually molested her when she was 13 years old. I also interviewed the uncle. In the Family Court report I offered an opinion about the likelihood of abuse and the risk the uncle posed to another child. At the trial the uncle was not called as a witness (a critical oversight by the lawyers) and the girl became so upset that her evidence was terminated by agreement. In the stand I had to disregard what each of these witnesses had told me during the assessment. After leaving out the interviews with the perpetrator and victim, there was not much to base a risk assessment on. This may not be perceived as fair but as explained in the beginning of this book, court is not about our everyday sense of fairness, it is about a set of rules applied to a particular case.

The fourth area of challenge in the cross-examination is to identify defects in the reasoning process. The opposing lawyer now wants you to justify your conclusions on the basis of the evidence. It is important that you have outlined the logic you used to come up with your opinion. In effect, the approach should be shown in the data; how you reached this particular inference and what alternatives there are. As the judge will have to provide a reason for their decision, so the court needs a reason for your opinion.

This is an area where many health professionals become unstuck. They outline what they did and found, then offer opinions without explaining the link. The court needs to understand your line of logic in reaching a conclusion. So you need to show A – B – C, not A – C. They have to see middle step B – the inferences. It is not enough to say, "it is my opinion" unless you can explain why that opinion came about. Recently a colleague who was the court expert in a Family Court matter had a judge refuse to accept his report as evidence. The judge argued that he appeared to have made appropriate enquiries and had reached opinions. However, the colleague had not explained how he reached the opinions so the judge could not accept the report. The trial was halted and my colleague had to rewrite the report.

The final aspect of the cross examination is not an attack although it may seem that way after the other processes. This aspect is for the lawyer to draw out evidence helpful to their own client. In effect they are going to say that maybe you are inadequately qualified, highly biased and made a whole bundle of mistakes in collecting your evidence, but you at least got these aspects right about their client!

I would point out that the lawyer in court may not follow the order given above, but in any good cross-examination, I would expect to see aspects of each of those five strategies. Hopefully, by understanding what the lawyer is trying to achieve, it will not seem so personal.

Re-examination

After the intense pressure of the cross-examination the initial lawyer is able to do a re-examination of you. They are not allowed to introduce new information but they can do a bit of damage control on issues raised during the cross-examination. Usually, this is quite brief and is over before you know it.

The process explained above is the standard case where there are two sides. However, there are times when there may be more than two sides. I had a Supreme Court trial where five men had been charged with rape. Each had legal representation. This meant four cross-examinations by the parties' counsels and one by the public prosecutor. Similarly, the Family Court often has more than two sides. The mother and father may both be legally represented, the children may have had their own lawyer appointed, there might be some grandparents who have a lawyer, and a welfare agency may be an intervener. It can get complicated but the procedures are basically the same.

In certain circumstances a judge may ask questions directly to the witness. In criminal and civil courts it is unlikely that the judge would ask many questions directly of you as the process is strictly adversarial, but they might direct the lawyers to ask certain questions. In the Family Court, and some children's courts, they have a different sort of mandate (usually because they are based on an enquiry model) so it is not uncommon for a Family Court judge to ask specific, and at times biting, questions. Usually, after questioning by a judge, the lawyers are asked if they want to clarify anything as the judge is not usually allowed to introduce new information.

The Judgment

After the testing has taken place, the judge or magistrate usually makes findings of fact about the information given and then applies the relevant law to those facts. This process is called a judgment. Judgments may be handed down immediately after all the evidence has been heard but often the decision is reserved until the judge can review all the information and formulate a reason for the decision. These situations may result in the judgment being handed down weeks or months after a trial.

Anyone who has done statistics as part of their study will quickly realise that the concept of judgment makes sense. In statistics there are probability levels. Generally, this is whether the alpha level is set to .01 or .05. Underlying the theory of probability is the knowledge that we cannot test if something is true, we can only test how likely the result occurred not by chance. The same process applies in court. A judge rarely knows if something really happened as he or she was not there. He or she can only infer the likelihood that an event took place with a degree of certainty.

In the criminal court, the standard of proof is called beyond reasonable doubt. The judge has to be really sure something happened. The risk of making the wrong decision is severe as someone could lose their right to freedom. Hence, the level is set so that it is better that ten guilty individuals go free rather than one innocent person be locked up. While the public do not like the concept of guilty people going free, it is actually addressing the statistical problem of Type I and Type II errors.

In other courts, the cost of a mistake is seen as less severe than the loss of freedom. In almost every other court my understanding is that the level is based on the balance of probabilities. The judge has to be more sure than not, that something is true. In a crude sense, they need to be 51 per cent sure that it happened, rather than 95 per cent sure in the criminal court.

The different probability levels can create interesting dilemmas. One example was a case before the family court where the father was alleged to have sexually abused his stepdaughter. He was charged by the police and went to trial in the District Court. After hearing the evidence the District Court judge found him 'not guilty' on the evidence they had. However, on the basis of the Family Court trial, he was a found to be high risk to the child. This in effect meant they found him 'guilty'. The man was upset because he felt he had been tried twice for the same crime. From a legal perspective, underlying this issue is that acquittal does not mean innocence. It means that the standard of proof was not met.

As a lay person we want to believe court is about truth. We want all the guilty people locked up and the innocent to go free. We want the right to prevail. As previously stated, court is not about absolute truth; it is about law and rules of evidence leading to justice.

Communication with Lawyers

I have had considerable contact with lawyers including running training for lawyers. As a result I am interested in the thought process of lawyers. I have observed that lawyers communicate in terms of evidence and fact. Lawyers love their facts and they want logic. Mental health professionals are less concerned about objective reality; they are interested in motive, emotion and dynamics. Therefore there are two very distinct views or, in other terms, different narratives. The medical doctor is more likely to be interested in fact, e.g. whether a disease is present or absent, but the language used to communicate this fact is still a very different narrative than that used by the lawyer.

I remember the moment when this insight hit home. It was in the middle of a trial for a young man diagnosed as suffering from bi-polar disorder. In his manic state he had stolen a car, and he was driving to Sydney to fly to America to take over the jaguar car factory because his name was similar. The factory was not in America, let alone New York, and why he had to drive to Sydney to fly to America he could not tell me. But the prosecutor said to me: "The fact of the matter is it not, is that he is a 17 year old in a stolen car, caught out of Kalgoorlie? I replied with an obvious "yes" to which the prosecutor replied "and how does that prove he has got bi-polar disorder?" The fact of the matter was that he was driving a stolen car. What I was interested in was the intent. Fortunately, the judge was also interested in intent and, at the end of the day, I helped the judge understand that it was likely that it was the bi-polar disorder which had motivated the young man's actions.

These patterns of communication are similar to male to female communication documented in the popular literature such as in John Gray's *Men are from Mars, Women are from Venus*. Lawyers taking the more factually based 'male' style while the mental health professional tends to use the emotive 'female' style. What we are dealing with are two systems of communication. In psychotherapy, there has been an increasing interest in Narrative Therapy and how the dominant narrative wins the communication conflict. Unfortunately, what happens is that when we talk to lawyers in court they are the dominant narrative. If we use our counselling skills we can understand that all we are doing is communicating with someone who communicates in a different way. The path to better understanding becomes clear. Logic, fact and reason are the language of legal process and we must work in the narrative.

My first lawyer friend was a lady by the name of Kate Stockwell. I used to ring her up at work sometimes, and she would be in 'lawyer-mode'. Her abrupt manner seemed cold and harsh. The phone call was simply "yes, yes, and no", click!

Afterwards I would think "what have I done to upset her?" It was as if this friendly chatty woman I knew had now been possessed by an alien. With time, I stopped personalising her reactions and came to realise that all she was doing was dealing with facts in the business-like manner of a lawyer. It is important to understand if you are talking to a lawyer, and you are waffling about emotional stuff, you will have lost them. Think through the facts and present them first. If you think they need the warm fuzzy stuff, give it to them after the business.

Another issue of the communication issue is highlighted in the following example. I was involved in a Care and Protection Hearing in the Children's Court in Western Australia. I had to wait for another psychologist to give evidence. As I had been appointed as expert in the Children's Court, I was allowed to sit in the back of the court and watch this other psychologist give evidence (normally witnesses have to wait outside). The psychologist had done some psychometric testing and was discussing the fact that the elevations were indicative of somatic complaints. The lawyer said to her: "What does this test profile mean when the client was stressed?" The psychologist replied "It would most likely result in somatic complaints". The lawyer said: "You mean complaints against the welfare department?" She was really nervous and said: "Yes, and the client will have physical illnesses". In that little interaction, the court and the two lawyers were left thinking that somatic complaints originated from some sort of sick litigious person who was going to sue government departments when stressed. The witness seemed like quite a sensible practitioner but because she was nervous and she was speaking a jargon which the court did not understand, the court was misled. Fortunately, I came along after her and was able to correct the misunderstanding. Whatever jargon you use, whether medical, psychological, from the social sciences, or accounting, be extremely careful to ensure that correct meanings are conveyed.

If you are ever in the position to realise that you are unintentionally misleading the court, it is appropriate for you to say: "I think my answers have been misleading the court". This is a line which gets them to stop in their tracks as the court does not want to be misled. If you then say, "look, sorry but I feel that I am creating a misunderstanding, can I clarify that answer?" usually the lawyer who was asking you the question will say "no" as they are happy with your answer but the other side usually jumps up and says "yes, we need to hear what he or she has got to say". As judges need to be informed, they may add their sway to get the situation clarified. Even if you do not get to clarify your position, the judge will know that you made a mistake and will consider that when they weigh up the evidence.

Rules of Evidence

Rules of evidence are principles of law which determine what may or may not be allowed to be given as evidence in court. There are whole law books on rules of evidence, as it is a complex area of law. As such, detailed understanding requires legal advice. However, I will provide my perspective to help explain certain aspects of these rules and to help highlight areas where you may need to seek legal advice.

A simple example to start with is a hypothetical case where someone called Rod comes into a seminar room in which I am conducting a workshop, trips over the power cord to my project and damages his hip in the fall. After running up $10,000 of medical expenses, missing a month of work, and being told he will never play professional football again, he sues me, and the hotel, for negligence. Everyone at the workshop who saw what happened is now a potential witness. In court these types of people are the best witnesses as they saw what happened. This is evidence from the direct observers – they are witnesses of fact. A fact in a legal sense is something which is directly perceived through one of the five senses. Normally, in court, the only person allowed to give evidence is someone who is a witness of fact. In giving evidence, such witnesses are not allowed to offer a reason why Rod fell. To say the power cord was wrongly placed or Rod was clumsy are opinions. Opinion evidence can only be given by people deemed to have expertise over and beyond normal people. This select group are the experts.

Suppose you were at my workshop and went home after seeing the fall. You excitedly say to your spouse: "Wow, something amazing happened today. This participant Rod came running in, tripped over a power cord, hurt himself, left in an ambulance and now he is suing everybody. I may have to go to court as a witness of fact". If your partner was called to court, he or she did not see the fall directly. They only know what you told them. Their evidence would be called hearsay. There are some very significant implications for hearsay evidence. For example, if you were assessing a child and spoke to the mother, and the mother does not give evidence, anything told to you by the mother could be disallowed as hearsay.

Steffen v Ruban (1966) is a precedent which is still cited. It is from New South Wales and illustrates this principle about admissibility of evidence. This case is where a medical doctor expressed opinions partly derived from what he had been told by the mother of the child and partly from the child (the child is the complainant). The mother was called as a witness but was too emotionally affected to give any more than brief evidence of the child's condition. The child was not called as a witness to the court. The case judgment notes:

> It cannot be clear from Dr Bailey's evidence whether he was expressing conclusions based on his own observations or based on what he had been told by the boy's mother. If his conclusions were mainly based on what he had been told by

the boy's mother then there is no evidence from her that what she had told the doctor was correct, and in the present case this is of vital importance. If any part of Dr Bailey's evidence was sufficiently clear, based on his own observations or tests, one could say that, despite deficiencies in the proof of the history of the child, the medical evidence was clear nevertheless, and there is no reason to interfere with the verdict. However, I find it quite impossible to say this on Dr Bailey's evidence.

So the situation here is that Dr Bailey was not clear on what information he got from the mother and what he got from the child. His Honour concluded: "If his evidence is such that it's impossible to analyse what the conclusions are based on his own observations and what the conclusions are based on what he had been told, then in such a case as the present one, the danger of mistrial becomes very great".

The implications from this judgment are twofold. The first is that if someone tells you something and that person is not going to court as a witness, that piece of information may not be admissible evidence. If it is not admissible in evidence, you cannot use it to offer an opinion in your assessment. The second is to make it very clear in your report what you directly hear, observe or test, and what comes from somewhere else, including documents and third party witnesses. If Dr Bailey had made it clear which parts of the information had been from the mother and from the child, then the judge may have been able to make a decision. Unfortunately, the judge could not tell so he had no choice but to order another trial.

Two examples of my own experiences in what seemed like good evidence dissolving to hearsay come from the Family Court. One was where I spoke to a child's principal at school and was told information. The classroom teacher, and not the principal, was called to give evidence at the trial and her evidence was nearly opposite to what I had been told by the principal. I had to disregard everything I had been told by the principal and change my opinions in light of what the teacher told me. No easy task in the middle of a cross-examination. In the second example, I interviewed a 19 year old who allegedly had been sexually abused by her uncle when she was 13 years old. I had spoken to the uncle. At the trial the uncle was not called as a witness. The young lady became too upset to give evidence and the court made a decision not to hear from her. Despite having a partial confession and detailed witness statement I was instructed to disregard that evidence as the court did not hear from either witness. It can be heartbreaking to know what I believed to be the truth but not be able to express it because of these rules of evidence. From my perspective if seems very unfair. However, in terms of legal process, for a judge to make a decision without proper evidence, the process would be legally unfair.

At the risk of being repetitive, when you write your report draw clear distinctions between what is an observation, what is your reasoning, and what are your opinions. I use lots of terms like "it is my opinion", and "it is my understanding". I avoid the term "I believe" as it is not an act of faith, nor do I use terms like "best guess" as guessing will not assist a court.

Judge Wisbey states:

> In order to facilitate a proper appreciation of the opinion and a sound evaluation of that opinion and its validity, it is essential that facts upon which the opinion are based are clearly identified. This then enables the application of common sense and logic to be used to determine the validity of the opinion. The application of forensic logic should generally provide the answer. It is important to indicate clearly in any report or evidence the part of the report or evidence based on fact, and which is inferential.

Expert Evidence

Judge Wisbey states: "Opinion evidence (that is the opinion of a witness as to the facts) is generally inadmissible." As mentioned earlier, most witnesses cannot have an opinion, they can only report on the fact of what they have perceived through their senses. He continues on to say:

> It is for the trial judge to draw all the necessary inferences or conclusions from the evidence presented...Opinions by experts are an exception to the general rule to which I have referred. Expert evidence 'is admissible whenever the subject matter of the enquiry is such that inexperienced persons are unlikely to prove capable of forming a correct judgment upon it without such assistance, in other words, when it so far partakes of the nature of a science as to require a course of previous habit, or study, in order to the attainment of a knowledge of it.

It is very important that if you are giving evidence, you do not overstep your area of expertise. The minute you start offering opinions on things that are based on lay understanding, you have ceased to be an expert offering an opinion. However, you may be called to offer opinions on medications when you are not medically trained, offer opinions on bruise patterns when you do not have a degree in injury patterns, to or discuss theories of attachment when your experience is with adults. If possible, recognise when you are being asked to cross the line.

There are three conditions, Judge Wisbey states, which must be fulfilled before evidence can be received as expert evidence. The first is "a witness cannot qualify as an expert unless his profession, habit or course of study or experience gives him a greater capacity of judging the issue than is possessed by other people." The person giving the evidence must demonstrate that he or she has the necessary qualifications to speak about the subject matter. I was asked to give evidence in a rape trial on a person who had suffered a brain injury as a child and was a heavy marijuana smoker. I was going to give evidence on the effects of marijuana smoking on brain injury and some of the implications. It was decided that expert psychological evidence was not necessary because the ordinary people of the jury were capable of judging that issue. The court was of the opinion that the normal person in the street knows enough about brain injury and marijuana use to make good judgments. While talking about habit, I found this anecdote a really fascinating example of being able to provide expert evidence: "A heroin addict has been held, by reason of experience in dealing with what is purported to be heroin, to be sufficiently equipped to offer an opinion as to whether a particular substance was heroin." So a heroin addict is an expert on heroin, because of their previous habit. They are only going to be able to give a very limited range of opinion evidence.

The second factor of Judge Wisbey is that "the qualifications or expertise must relate to a matter which is capable of being the subject of expertise-- that is of training and/or experience placing the person possessing it in a position to form an educated opinion on the matter not capable of being formed by persons generally". This is self-explanatory.

The third factor in regards to expert evidence is that "no expert is entitled to deal with the question, the answer to which ultimately depends upon an application of legal standard". This is referring to the ultimate issue which was discussed in the previous chapter.

If you can gain one thing from this book, then this is the point to remember: "Courts look to experts for well-grounded opinions based on scientific neutrality, rather than disguised personal preferences or speculation" (McCann & Dyer, 1996, p. 34). If your position is scientifically neutral, you will be a good expert. The more you align to an outcome, a position, or a person, the less favourably your evidence will be perceived by the court. I read somewhere a quote which stated words to the effect of "the perfect expert is someone who has no investment in any particular outcome".

One of our State forensic pathologists gave a great example at a forensic college meeting about DNA testing. She said she does not know who the samples belong to and she does not care. All she cares about is the probability that two samples are the same or different. If you can master the position of being a computer of variables related to your area of expertise, then you will do well in court. If you want to become rigid and dig-your-feet-in then you will do very badly.

Judge Wisbey provides another way of describing that same key point: "It is essential that the expert remains impartial to the cause, and appreciates that his or her obligation is to the truth (the court) rather than the party who has engaged them". When you are in court, you work for the court not a client. Your role is to provide truth to a judge, so that they can make a decision. This may bring up some ethical issues because, in many professions, the ethical standard explicitly states that the practitioner has an over-riding obligation to the client. However, knowing what the court expects allows you to structure your presentation to accommodate the competing needs. Most inexperienced professionals do not understand their obligation to the court as expert witnesses and create frustration and confusion for both themselves and the court.

American expert witnesses have become known in the *University of Chicago Law Review* as 'saxophones', because the attorneys play the tune, manipulating the expert to make the sounds they want! You do not want to be known as a saxophone, as it is the opposite of what makes a good expert. You do not want to be manipulated. Lawyers do play games and they try to get evidence to support their position. However, I have a reputation for impartiality and I hang on to that reputation with as much vigour as I can. If I am asked to do a second opinion report, and I come back with something which is contrary to what the lawyers are hoping, I still say it. I may try to write it in a way where it is beneficial for their position in court, but I try not to get sucked into writing something for the sake of getting more referrals.

There are professionals who are happy to work for just one side of a dispute. These are the so-called 'hired guns'. In every profession, there are people who have set positions. When you hear they have done a report, even without reading it, you already know what their findings will be. I find this position reprehensible. All cases are different and each case should be on its own merit leading to its own outcome. The one-sided position generates income but in my opinion those practitioners have sold out their professional integrity and are causing damage to the reputation of the wider profession. Where it is possible, I try to do some work for both sides of the situation. I would like to work for defence and prosecution, insurer and claimant, or offender and victim. It helps to stay balanced. Unfortunately, it is not always possible. For example, in Western Australia, prosecution reports are generally done in-house while the defence uses outsourced experts.

Impartiality has implications for attending court. What I find statistically is that one in ten of my independent and comprehensive Family Court reports end up in a trial. In reality this means I rarely go to court even when I am dealing with serious allegations occurring in complex situations. If I give party evidence by working for just one side or the other, I would estimate that somewhere around five in ten go to trial. Therefore, the better your report, and the more objective you are perceived to have been, the less frequently the report will be challenged.

Perhaps the most important aspect to consider is with whom does the role of advocacy belong in the courtroom? A lawyer is the advocate for the client in the courtroom, not you. You are an advocate for the profession and truth but not the client.

Acting as a Reliable Witness

The expert functioning as a reliable witness will operate on a number of dimensions. These include the following:

Neutral versus Partisan

Are you seen as a seeker of the truth or are you just confirming a position? Lawyers get to know your position very quickly, and if you have a pattern of findings you will be labelled accordingly. Obviously the truth seeker will be seen in a much better light.

In speaking about the tendency for witnesses to become partisan Judge Wisbey states: "It is important not to lose sight of the fact that a conflict in expert's views reflecting genuine differences of opinion based upon the then state of the Psychological Science, and perhaps reflecting patient's presentation, is an important part of the adversarial system." Judges can see that we do not have to agree with each other. Just because someone has a different view, it does not mean it is wrong.

Objective versus Subjective

Are you offering a reasoned opinion argued on evidence, or are you basing it on personal preferences and opinions? If you are objective you will do well in court but if you are subjective then you deserve to get shot down in court.

Flexible versus Rigid

Does the opinion change with hypothetical and other information? When I first started out, I used to dig in my heels when asked hypothetical propositions. I would say: "Oh, no, that didn't happen", that is, I would argue whether or not the hypothetical happened. What I learned is if you preface the answer but address their question you are seen in a much better light: "I found no evidence of that, but if it happened this would be my opinion." You have now become the computer adjusting expert variables. This is critically important because if you come into the trial on day three, you will not know what has happened in the first two days. You may be asked to consider something hypothetically which then turns out to be real.

Judge Wisbey describes this point in the following quote:

> There are often occasions when an expert, confronted during his or her evidence with material of which he or she was not previously aware, will not be prepared to acknowledge that it has any relevance or impact on his or her opinion. It is important that you are prepared to accommodate new material and to acknowledge that it impacts upon your opinion if that is the case. A witness should not be frightened to indicate to the trial judge that he or she would need time to reflect on the new material before indicating whether or not it affects the opinion that has been expressed.

Co-operative versus Defensive

I heard about a colleague whom I did not know very well, arguing with a judge when he challenged the subpoena to produce his counselling notes. The therapist argued: "I don't want to show you my notes", to which the judge replied, "well you have to". The therapist then said "but it's confidential".

The judge seemingly unimpressed with this argument said: "I have ordered you to show me your notes, if you do not I can gaol you for contempt of court". The therapist foolishly replied, "but no, they're confidential"! This is an unwise stance as it will not help his evidence one iota. He had lost any credibility he may have had due to a lack of understanding of the law. If he had understood he was there to assist the court, he could have expressed concerns about confidentiality and then handed over the notes, having fulfilled any ethical obligation he felt about releasing confidential information.

Sells Time versus Opinion

A hired gun is someone who has opinions for sale. Everyone knows what they will write and the market seeks those opinions. This may result in short-term gains for an individual but damages the credibility of the entire profession. A reliable witness is someone who sells time. they conduct a thorough assessment and provide reasonable opinions. The opinion remains the same, no matter which side pays for it.

4

GOING TO COURT

This chapter addresses some of the practical issues involved in going to court. As explained throughout this book, the material presented can only give a generic approach. Make sure you find out the specifics of any local protocols for a particular court.

Court Dates and Times

Lawyers work on the principle of billable units of time. This means that they do not want to do things which are unnecessary as it costs. If they are preparing for a court appearance they will read all the documents close enough to the event to remember the material. If they read them a month in advance, they have to read them a second time near the appearance, which uses up precious time and costs someone money. The implication of this is that they will study the case close to the time resulting in a mad flurry of activity at what seems to us to be the last minute. They read the material and find gaps in the case so they seek further reports and other information. As it is now close to the court date, it means that everything is urgent. I had a lawyer recently telephone on a Wednesday with a request for a report by the Friday.

In the procedural rules of court, there are periods of time where documents have to be filed before a trial. Typically, all of the parties send their information in 21 days before (obviously it depends on the rules of the particular court). This may be the first time that both sides see all the reports and documents. This then allows them to make decisions to settle the case as they can see how weak or strong their case may really be. Often during the last few days before a trial, and sometimes even during a trial, the parties reach agreement.

The consequence is that trials often fall through at the last minute. In my experience, for every three trial dates I write in the planner, two will settle. That means I have to operate like the lawyers and save my preparation to near the trial date. I may not charge billable minutes but my time is my product and it is not reusable!

It also pays not to allow yourself to become too anxious about a pending trial as more often than not it does not happen. This does not mean that you do not collect the material together in preparation; it means you do not spend too long studying it before the time you need to give the evidence. For example, if I am not sure of the current literature I may pay a student to research the current material on a topic, or I may search the Internet, but I do not study it in detail until the last few days.

When you get instructions about going to court, make sure that you find out when they want you to attend. Professional people often can get 'interposed' (put in by agreement even if it is contrary to the normal order of proceedings) at a convenient time. If you are an officer of the court like a court counsellor, and in some jurisdictions, any type of a public servant, you may not have a choice. You may be required when the court wants you.

If you have a choice, there are appearance times which are more effective. Various courts start at different times but usually it is somewhere between 9.30 and 10.15 am. Occasionally, a court will start earlier. If you can, see if you can give your evidence first up in the morning. I find that as the day goes on, the likelihood of the court running late increases. However, if I cannot be the first witness of the day, first witness after lunch is not a bad time. Times like 11.30 am and 3.30 pm are almost always going to run late so bring something to read.

Most judges are reasonable people who will try to accommodate the professional person, especially if they are aware of special circumstances. I have been involved in cases where they have altered times to accommodate me. For example, I was in the country and the judge asked if I could give my evidence on the next day as they were not likely to get through the other witnesses before 5 pm and she wanted me to give my evidence last. I explained that my wife was at home with six-week-old baby twins and that I had booked to fly back at 8 pm that night. The judge kindly offered to have the court sit until 7.30 pm if necessary to finish the evidence and get me on the flight home. I have had judges go through lunch breaks, start court early, and go over time to ensure that my evidence was finished so I did not have to come back. On the other hand, I have also had judges stop at 4.30 pm on the dot and require that I come in for just ten minutes the next day. It depends on the judge, but if you do not let your needs be known, then there is no chance of you getting your needs met. So if you have a special need, let the briefing lawyer know, or speak to the judge and see what happens. It is important to express your appreciation when they do vary the process to accommodate you as they do not have to make any allowance and they can require you sit outside the courtroom until they need you!

The Family Court in Western Australia have a system of a 'not before date'. They say the trial is not before the 14th April, which means it could be the 15th or the 16th or the 17th. The reason for this is it is not good for judges to be sitting around idle when there is a backlog of cases. As many Family Court matters settle, the system needs a way of dropping settled cases without leaving gaps, so they bank up pending trials. Civil trials tend to have a specific date and that date is fixed for many months.

Before setting a trial date, the lawyers should approach their witnesses and ask if there are any times when they are not available to give evidence. The usual request is something like: "Can you please advise us of your unavailable dates for the months of...?" Once advised, they should then ensure that the trial is held at a time when you are available. Obviously, unavailable dates are about substantial absences such as interstate trips, major training events, and the like. I generally do not worry about single days when I may not be available as usually it is possible to work around it (unless the matter is a short-listed hearing of only one day). It is when I am not available for two or more days that I consider listing myself as unavailable for a trial.

Giving Evidence

Most lawyers will want to know what you are going to say. One of principles of good cross-examination is to never ask a question you do not know the answer to. Therefore most briefing lawyers (the one who got you involved in the first place) will want to talk to you about your evidence. I will always try to talk to the lawyer about what they are going to ask me about. Do note that there are protocols of what a lawyer may be able to tell you and even whether they can talk to you. The general rule is that a briefing lawyer is the one who can talk to you.

There are two main ways of doing this. I will either telephone the briefing lawyer and/or trial barrister a few days in advance or I ask to meet them half an hour before I give evidence (I meet them outside the courtroom). I generally make notes of what they are going to ask me so I can think about my response. Do realise that they will also be taking note of your answers to see if it is worth asking the questions on the day. Do not feel intimidated by this process as it is a 'warm up' for when you get to court. On more than one occasion I have had a lawyer telephone and request a list of questions I want to be asked. Better still, I have been asked to look at another professional's report and provide a list of questions for the lawyer to ask. This type of request is rare but interesting.

It is important to remember that in the lead up to the trial, legal practitioners have had access to all the information and they have probably tried to reach some sort of settlement. The entire documents have been filed so they know what the other side has got. They know what the sticking points are after they have been to the conciliation meetings. If they will tell you what the other side is going to ask you, you can prepare in advance. Over time I have come to realise that what I think may be relevant to the trial is not necessarily what the lawyers consider relevant. Therefore I will ask my briefing lawyer what the other side may want to ask me.

If you ask this type of question be careful about privilege. As described earlier, there are rules of law which protect communications between a briefing lawyer and client. A lawyer may not be able to answer certain questions. How much the lawyer can tell you is a product of the nature of your involvement. As a court expert you may be told much, while as a subpoenaed witness you may not be told anything at all. My advice is ask, it is the lawyer's job to know what is privileged.

In terms of etiquette, I do not seek information from parties who have not briefed me at some point of the process. I certainly would not ring an opposing barrister and ask what they are going to ask me. If a party is self-represented, the situation is much harder. This is a problem generally reserved for the family court where custody cases may take place with one or both parties not having a lawyer. Discussions with someone who does not have legal representation can open you up to all sorts of problems and is best avoided wherever possible.

Another important consideration involves the timing of discussions with lawyers. Once you have started to give evidence in court, you must not talk to anyone about your evidence unless you are expressly told that you are permitted to do so. This applies whether you have a five-minute adjournment, overnight breaks in the evidence, or a split trial over weeks or months. Your evidence must be kept pure which is part of the reason why witnesses are not allowed to sit in court until after they have given evidence. Once your evidence is completed, unless otherwise stated, you can talk to various lawyers again (within the bounds of confidentiality, ethics, etc.).

Read All your Information

One of my worst experiences in court happened before a trial judge in the Family Court. It was a complicated trial. The trial was underway and I was to give evidence on the Thursday. On the Tuesday, a courier dropped off a large wad of documents which proved to be the grandmother's diary in this case. She had had the young child in her care for a number of months and had recorded everything. When I received the documents, I was having a very busy week (full days, evening meetings, etc.). The Thursday before court, I got up early and I read all the affidavits which had been filed, I read all my notes, my report, other reports, but I glanced through the diary.

I went into the trial and it started off really well but one of the lawyers said something like: "Dr Watts, in the diary provided by the grandmother..." and I said, "well, I have only just scanned it..." Then the judge stopped, and the lawyer stopped, everyone looked at the judge, and the judge said words to the following effect: "I consider that a very important piece of information. Are you saying, Dr Watts, that you have not read it?" I had to say "Yes, Your Honour". After what seemed like a huge pause he said, "you've got two choices. I can stop the trial now and resume it tomorrow after you have read it, or you can continue and give your evidence without having read this very significant piece of information", or words to that effect. The judge then adjourned for lunch while I considered my decision. I went back to a nearby lawyer's office, locked myself in and spent the next hour and a quarter reading all the documents I could possibly read. I then went back and explained what I had done. The judge sort of went "humph" and then the trial continued.

In his judgment, there were parts of my evidence which he liked but he was damning of the way I had dealt with that particular issue. While it was difficult for me to have read that material in the time I had, the judge was correct in his view that I should have read the material before giving evidence upon it. The moral of that story is that if it is sent to you, read it. It was an awful experience and one which could have been avoided.

Bringing Material to Court

One of the common questions I get asked is "what can I bring to court with me?" There may be an argument about what you can actually use at the time, but it is important to bring certain things. The most obvious item is the complete file related to the client. It is very rare that you will not be permitted to refer to your original notes and assessment data.

The deciding factor for the judge is whether there is a link between the recording of the notes and event in question. If you ask to look at the notes to 'refresh your memory' then it is probable as the implicit assumption is the notes contain the contemporaneous information needed to assist recall.

When you look though the notes, make sure they are in order and you know approximately where to find things. The use of small stick-on tags to highlight particular documents of significant is very handy. If you are obsessive, maybe colour code them so reports can be separated from test data and observations. Be aware, however, that anything you take into court and relied upon during your evidence can become part of the court records so it is important that you do not take anything in that you are not prepared to surrender if asked.

I will bring a folder I call my court file. The file is of course black because I want that formal look. In it I have copies of my current curriculum vitae, a full Resumé, and various items of potential use. I have reliability and validity scales of the Wechsler Tests (which I have never actually used but are there 'just in case'). I have some literature on recommended ages for overnight contact, Family Relations Test information, parental alienation information, judgments in a fitness to stand trial hearing where precedent law was set, indicators of sexual abuse, Kohlberg's stages of moral development and the list goes on. I will also take relevant references, such a DSM-IV if I know there is going to be an argument over a diagnosis or a particular issue. I take the file into court with me and if I get asked a really curly question I say: "I have some information with me, can I refer to it?" I find I have about an 80 per cent approval rate in the Family Court and 60 per cent in the criminal court. Different courts have slightly different rules but if it is there and you can use it, why not! Having the file with me also gives me something to read while I am waiting for court to commence.

A helpful hint is that if you copy something relevant, such as criteria for a particular personality disorder, medical diagrams, or other material, photocopy at least four copies for your file. You will look very professional if you have multiple copies to share around. If you had only one copy, you may end up waiting while the clerk goes off to another room to photocopy the document. While he or she is gone, everyone remains silently waiting for the return.

Court Room Procedures

Basic Etiquette

Arriving early to court is a good start. If you arrive late, you will not composed, calm, or have time to discuss things with the briefing lawyer. If you are very late, the judge may already be negative towards you for wasting everyone's time. Therefore, in the larger cities ensure you allow adequate time for traffic and parking.

If you have not been to court before, arrive half an hour early and ask for the lawyer to give you a quick look around. Alternatively, there are now web sites which enable you to have a virtual tour of a court room (for example see www.justice.wa.gov.au in Western Australia).

Courts vary slightly in design but they have basically the same format. The judge generally sits higher than everybody else. In front of the judge is usually the judge's associate. There is the bench where the lawyers and their clients sit facing the judge. At the back of the court is the gallery where spectators and people who have finished giving their evidence sit. At one side of the court room, near the judge, is the witness box where you will give evidence. There is generally an usher who sometimes sits on the side or sometimes roves around to different places.

In many courtrooms there is a little booth where they have a person monitoring the taping equipment which records the court proceedings. It is important to note that the microphone that is in the witness box is there to tape your evidence – it is not there for voice amplification, so make sure you speak loudly enough to be heard.

Your entry to court will be at one of two main times. Either court is waiting to start or alternatively court is in progress. If court has not started, you can walk in and introduce yourself to the lawyers (if possible, exchange pleasantries to both sides but certainly the briefing lawyer). Alternatively, at least meet the usher and introduce yourself. If the court is ready for your evidence, it is generally acceptable to sit at the back of the court until called (unless there are arguments about your evidence in which case wait outside until called). If court is in progress, it is normal for a witness to wait outside.

I would generally suggest that you look into court before entering (most courtrooms have a small window in the door) and make sure that a witness is not standing up as it may mean they are being sworn in. It is not appropriate to enter during the swearing in. However, if a lawyer is standing, then it is okay to quietly enter the court. In the case where the court is in session, I would open the door, catch the eye of the usher without entering the court, and then I would wait outside until I was called.

Court Rules are Formal

The legal profession is guided by variety of rules and customs which go back several hundred years. One custom which is generally protocol in all courts is that you bow to the judge. This happens each time the judge enters the court. Similarly, when you enter or leave the court, it is normal to briefly pause at the door and bow to the judge. No one will come after you for not doing it, but it looks professional if you do.

One rule which is strongly policed is the turning off of mobile phones. In this age of technology, a ringing phone is one of biggest breaches of etiquette you can commit in court. In some courts it is also considered rude to have your sunglasses on the top of your head so remember to take them off.

The use of correct titles in court is very important. An almost universal convention is that a judge is 'your honour', a magistrate is 'your worship'. 'Sir', 'madam' are common terms when you talk to anyone in court. Lawyers should be called by their surnames with the title 'Mr', 'Ms', 'Mrs' or 'Miss'. Children are generally called by their first names but adults by their title and surname. In the family court, it may be possible to call parties by their first names but if you are not sure, the safest line is to err on the side of formality.

Your Rights in Court

While you do not have many rights in court, you are entitled to be comfortable. For example, if you need a drink of water the usher will get you one. As it is common to get a dry mouth when nervous, a drink is a good idea. Having a drink can also be a strategy if you feel that your composure is going. Pause to have a drink, then answer.

Another right in court is to be able to understand the question. If the question catches you off guard, take a few moments to think before answering. If it reflects new information, it is possible, and indeed encouraged, for you to say, "can I think about that for a few moments before answering?" If a question is long, it is possible to ask for it to be rephrased if you do not understand. If the question has multiple parts then ask that they be addressed one at a time. If a lawyer asks a particularly long question, simply asking for it to be repeated can be a good strategy – if a lawyer is not reading questions from their notes, they may not be able to repeat it.

Hopefully, you will have remembered to go to the toilet before giving your evidence but if you need a toilet break it is appropriate to ask by using the politest terms possible. Be warned that the judge may choose to stop for lunch because of the request, so if you are nearly finished, hang on! What starts out as a five-minute stop may become an hour-and-a-half break.

Another bit of advice I discovered through hard experience is never take a medication you are not familiar with. Fortunately, my experience was related to a mock trial for training purposes. I had a horrible head cold so I had taken a couple of anti-cold tablets and cough mixture. As I was not used to the medication and was not well, I became quite faint. If I had been trying to give evidence and not reading a script, I would have had a real problem. If you are genuinely ill, please let the court know as early as possible and ensure you get a medical certificate to prove that you had a real illness. Calmative medications such as benzodiazepines are not recommended unless they are your usual prescription medication.

Demeanour

This word is not a word commonly used by the health profession but would be something a lawyer may use. The reason is simple. Demeanour is about outward appearance. It fits with the legal principle of factual evidence being what can be seen or heard.

The first aspect of developing the appropriate demeanour is your appearance. Look like an expert in dress and manner. Judges are not only listening to what you are saying, they are also looking at how you come across as you say it. I had a case where another psychologist had been attacking my report and I felt she had been quite personal in her attack. When I was giving evidence, I was asked to make comment about her critique of my report. Due to the emotion associated with the issue, I went on about her critique. An experienced barrister who was present said to me afterwards: "Phil, why did you even go there? You should have just rolled your eyes back, given a big sigh and with a look of contempt implied why bother with this woman?" I am not sure I would be prepared to play the game to that level but that is how that barrister considered it should be played.

The dress aspect of demeanour is also important. Irrespective of how you look in your office, court is formal. When I am in court, I am always in a suit, unless I am called on an urgent and unexpected basis to give evidence (which generally should not occur). In some courts the dress expectations for female witnesses can be old-fashioned. I have heard of a female lawyer arriving to court dressed in trousers and being told to change. Hopefully, that was a rare event in these enlightened times. It may pay to discuss local protocol with your lawyer if you are in doubt. However, what is not in doubt is the need to power dress.

A calm presentation is important but this is not always easy to achieve in a high-stress environment associated with giving evidence in court. Anyone in the mental health area is likely to have done training in relaxation skills and anxiety management techniques. We teach these techniques to our anxious clients but when it comes time to go to court, we seem to forget how to apply the techniques to ourselves. If you are feeling anxious, remember the basic breathing techniques such as breathing out slowly while thinking the word 'calm'. You can also have a sip of water or pause to think about an answer. It may help to remember that we do not want to remove all anxiety. The inverted U relationship between anxiety and performance means that an optimum level of arousal is needed to achieve peak performance.

The demeanour should not extend to the point of being arrogant or defensive. I had a case where I was asked to watch a video I had taken and see if I agreed with the statement from my report that the girl was pointing to her vagina. On watching the video it was not clear whether the girl was pointing to her leg or her vagina. I tried the approach: "It doesn't matter what I think now, the video is here for the judge to decide". That did not wash with the judge and in his reason for decision he said I was defensive. The lesson from the experience is that if you make a mistake, it is better to own up to it than become defensive. Advice from David Childs, a leading Perth Family Court barrister in this regard is, "if you have to give ground or make a concession, do so! It is not unusual for this to happen and it is better to make the concession rather than stick to a lost point".

If the arguments are complex try to give both sides of the story. The biggest threat to presenting two sides to the story is the yes/no questioning. If you watch American law shows on television they play the position that everything can only be answered yes or no. My experience is that occasionally you get Australian lawyers who say "just answer the question, yes or no", but mostly they will let you have your say. There are various ways of dealing with someone who challenges you with the yes/no approach. I have two strategies which are frequently helpful. One is when I am getting a lot of yes and no questions, I say "if I answer that question with a yes or no answer it would be misleading to the court" and usually the court does not want to be misled so they allow you to answer the question. The other one is going with the yes/no questions until they lead you to their grand proposition. When it is given, answer the opposite to what is expected but do not elaborate until requested. When requested, say: "I will if you will let me explain".

Your demeanour should also reflect the position discussed in the section about expert evidence. You are not advocating for a client but assisting the court.

Occasionally you may be questioned about a particular article or your knowledge of the literature. It is important that you do not let this fluster you. How you handle the question depends on your knowledge of the literature. If it is an area where you are clearly comfortable, it probably does not matter. However, if they have referred you to an area which perhaps you should have known about but which you do not, then you are in serious trouble. If the case is potentially going to enter a literature debate I will often ring one of my colleagues who specialises in the area so I can get a current review article of the key material relevant to the issue.

There are a few doctors, psychologists and social workers with law degrees and practising as lawyers so the unexpected can happen. They are probably the most dangerous people you could meet in court because they actually know what they are asking you about. Most times lawyers ask a few half-hearted questions to see how you respond. If you flinch, they will go for the jugular. If you stand your ground, they will usually back off, especially when they get into areas like testing. It is very easy to baffle them if you want to. I have been stressing throughout this book not to use jargon. This is the one time when you use jargon. For example, if told that a test is not valid, respond with "which type of validity are you referring to – construct, criterion, or some of the other forms of validity?"

Costing

Those in the public sector are likely to have to attend court for their normal pay. The department they work for may be able to claim the cost of the lost time but if they do, the worker will not see the money. In private practice, the recommended fee set by professional bodies is generally higher than the normal hourly rate. This is because attending court is seen as requiring added expertise and actually attending court interferes with the normal running of the practice. For example, the APS recommends a rate at 1.5 times the standard fee.

The most common problems in regards to payment for attending court stem from a failure to recognise that you need to negotiate a fee for service PRIOR to attending court. Some courts may have prescribed payments for the attendance but most do not. Areas such as workers' compensation are more likely to have fee schedules for expert witnesses. In these cases, local knowledge of costing is required. In other cases, the legal profession understands that services should be reimbursed. However, it is not up to the lawyer to determine how much you should be paid.

I consider a request to attend court to be a contract which needs to be negotiated prior to providing the service. It is an issue which should be dealt with by writing back to confirm attendance times, fees and your cancellation policy. If it is in writing, then everyone knows where they stand and the legal professional can allow for the funds to be held in trust for your payment and, if necessary, to vary the arrangement with you.

An interesting consideration for some professions is the GST aspect. While you should get specific advice from a tax accountant, my understanding of the general principle is that treatment by a doctor or psychologist is a GST-exempt service (although 'counselling' may attract GST). Writing reports, assessment specifically for court, and giving evidence are not treatment so they are subject to GST. Therefore, do not forget to include this in the costing.

A cancellation clause needs to be included in any arrangement as court will often settle at the last minute. The issue you need to work out is your timeframe for cancellation fees. I do quite a lot of court work so I try to be reasonable and flexible about cancellations and changes. My normal policy is that that I usually have a 24-hour cancellation period where I require 50 per cent of the expected costs. Another aspect of cancellation is when the request is to give evidence in the morning but the appearance is changed to the afternoon on short notice. Some professionals charge, others just see it as part of the costs of going to court. The bottom line is to balance the need to be flexible in assisting the court against the costs to your practice.

In my confirmation letter I also give a minimum block of time of my availability. In what is expected to be a straightforward appearance, I state that I am available to the court for a two-hour minimum attendance (whether waiting or giving evidence) plus travel time. In complex matters I often state three hours. I also indicate the per hour rate for each additional hour.

In the case where it is a country matter, I may only be in court for a short time but I have to charge for how long I am away from my practice. This may be a whole day plus travel expenses. In some States telephone linkups are used in country matters. I prefer to give evidence in person but I understand the need to balance cost against my preference. If I am a central party in a complex matter I insist in giving live evidence. If I am a minor party I may give telephone evidence. I would charge for how long I am available, not how long I am on the telephone.

Another thing you need to think about is the cost of preparation. I charge my standard assessment rate for preparation time. There may be a dispute about what are legitimate aspects of preparation. I allow a small preparation charge to reread the material in my file (it would be expected that I know this material already, so I do not believe it is appropriate to charge for a lot of this type of preparation). I charge an hourly rate to read anything else the lawyer sends me including other reports and trial affidavits. I do not normally charge for researching the literature unless the lawyer has requested a review. Knowing the literature is part of the role of being an expert.

Becoming a Better Expert

How do you become better in court? The answer is through using the experiences in court to give you feedback, as well as seeking ideas from other sources.

Feedback

One of the most powerful sources of information to give you feedback is the cross-examination. Lawyers ask questions because they did not understand a part of the report or they saw it as a weakness. If you can put your wounded ego aside and think about what they have cross-examined you on, you will learn about how the legal profession viewed your written evidence. If you go to court, and have your report admitted into evidence but the lawyers do not ask any substantive questions, consider your report to be well-written. Either the issues were so clear that they have accepted it as written, or they were so concerned about the implications, they did not want to touch it! Both options are a credit to how you approach the task, more so the former.

After a trial, a judge makes a judgment in which he or she explains how he or she as the ultimate user of the information viewed the witnesses' credibility and how it related to the relevant law. Just as we are expected to explain the factual base and inferences upon which our reports are based, the judge is also required to explain the basis of his or her decision. This is called a 'reason for decision'. A judge needs to do this so if their judgment is appealed, a higher court can consider the judge's reasons. These will be spoken verbally in court but also come out as a written document. Most lawyers would not think to send one to an expert witness, but are usually only too happy to if requested. I generally ask the briefing lawyer to send me a copy. It is one of the few times that you will ever get direct feedback about how a judge perceived your evidence.

Another source of information comes from the barristers who examined your evidence in court. If you ask them directly, or through the lawyer who briefed you, it may be possible to get some useful feedback. How much they say will depend partly on your relationship with them, and partly on their personality.

Develop your Skills

As has been emphasised throughout this book, it is imperative that you learn the rules of the game to deal effectively with court. To be a better expert you need to keep improving by learning the rules.

As with all academic skills, reading the literature is a useful approach. In the appended reference list, I cite a few examples of books in different areas of medico-legal process. The main comment I would make is to be discerning in the material studied. There is a mountain of literature available, however, much of it is American. I am not anti-American literature but I feel I should point out that America has a different court system which is much more adversarial. The American law shows on television have coloured many Australian professional's perceptions on what court may be like. When watching the shows, there is the sense of vicious challenges, verbal insults, and tricks to trip up the expert. In Australia that may happen, but on the basis of my experience, it is relatively rare. I have found that generally I have been treated with respect, not yelled at or berated as seen on television!

Professional associations generally provide information on dealing with courts. I am aware that the Australian Medical Association is proactive in informing its members of expert evidence issues. Psychology has been a bit tardy but recently there have been some good articles in the APS professional magazine *In Psych*. These have included dealing with subpoenas, the new Family Court Guidelines, and giving evidence in court. I have listed several of these in the reference list and if you have access to the member section of the web site, these are contained there.

An area of professional development of all health and allied health professionals should be training in all aspects of the legal process. I recently heard that the complementary medicine and para-medical areas are being called the 'cash cows of the new millennium' in terms of litigation. The context of the comment came in a discussion where it was said that medical doctors are getting too well defended and are protecting their assets more effectively. Other related professions are seen as poorly defended and ill-prepared for dealing with law suits. If we do not want to be milked, it is essential that we seek ongoing training and read literature to help us. As stated in the beginning, the more you know the rules of the game, the better you can survive the experience.

For want of a better name, court coaching is a useful strategy for improving performance in court. Some colleagues going off to court will call me to discuss the case in a supervision session. I am certain that all professions have experienced people willing to assist the less experienced. As long as confidentially is carefully guarded, and dual roles avoided, this can be tremendously helpful. Similar to the coaching, a debriefing session with an experienced colleague after giving evidence is useful in helping make an objective appraisal of the situation.

Underpinning the different methods listed above is doing whatever you can to improve your understanding of the legal system. It is important to realise that differing opinions are a necessary part of the adversarial system. It does not matter if you have a different opinion to your colleagues. What you have to ensure is that you have a sound opinion, based on good evidence. Judge Wisbey notes:

It's important that the expert avoids adopting the role of a trailblazer for untried or dubious theories. If the expert wishes to be adventurous (and perhaps that shouldn't be discouraged), it is important that he or she enunciates clearly the novelty of the view and identifies any opposing view.

Learning from My Mistakes

Even the most experienced court professional with a high regard within a profession can come unstuck. In a case like that it is important to analyse what happened so you can learn from your mistakes. I share the following example so you can also learn from my mistakes because it highlights the point that even with experience, there is no way to be infallible.

The following example is based on a Family Court case. Information of the family obviously needs to be kept to very general, non-specific details as it is not appropriate to release sensitive case-identifiable information. I also stress that the following represents my interpretation of the events and if you asked the judge or the various lawyers involved, they would have a different perception.

The case involved an assessment of issues to do with the welfare of one boy aged about ten years whose parents had separated when he was a baby. The parents had never seen eye to eye but had muddled through a combination of weekend and shared care arrangements. The father had been convicted of physically assaulting the boy some three years previously. He was not gaoled. He had resumed contact and gradually the mother let him look after the boy during the week and she looked after him at weekends. The father had a relationship break-up and various allegations of psychological and emotional harm to the boy were raised by the ex-girlfriend.

To my mind, the case started out as a very routine Family Court expert appointment. I was in that all important independent position and had the opportunity to do a full assessment which had involved more time than my standard Family Court assessment. It was a case where, when I interviewed the father, his own description of a number of events was extremely alarming from a psychological perspective. Consequently, I did not have to rely on making interpretations from what other parties had told me as his own evidence was a compelling indictment. There was also other independent evidence such as a previous conviction for physically assaulting the child and a police officer to whom the father had reported similar views (unfortunately the policeman was not called to give evidence as a witness at the trial).

I wrote a report. In the report I focussed on one particular episode of concerning behaviour, because I thought it was a cut and dried scenario, which would have alarmed anybody. However, as I thought it was such a clear-cut case, I did not consider my trial preparation as seriously as I should have. The lesson here is there is never a routine case; approach all cases like they are complex.

The father objected to my report, but certain recommendations had been followed. In particular, the child needed psychological counselling and the father needed a psychiatric assessment. The psychiatric report failed to find the same level of concern I had noted (I had been arguing of the possibility of either a delusional disorder or personality disorder). The psychiatrist came back with a view that the father lacked 'common sense' but was not psychiatrically ill or personality disordered. Unfortunately for me, I was not aware that the child had been referred to the recommended psychological counselling. I was provided with a copy of that report about ten minutes into my evidence! The court was adjourned shortly, to allow me to read it, but I did not have time to think through the implications. I offered the opinion that there was a certain degree of agreement between our reports, but because of the way the other report was written, that overlap did not come through. Herein lay one of my problems, and for future reference, if I am aware that someone is providing treatment I should follow up to see if a report was going to be provided to the court well before the trial.

As described earlier in this book, two sides of an argument are put before a judge to help the judge discern the situation. In this particular Family Court case, the father had engaged a noted Queen's Counsel. I had known the QC for a decade and he is an extremely good strategist (as one would expect from a QC). The mother, on the other hand, was unable or unwilling to finance legal representation and was representing herself. Consequently, at the trial, in terms of adversarial process, the father had a major advantage. In a case like this, where one party has legal representation and the other does not, it puts tremendous pressure on the expert to not only give evidence, but also to be able to help counterbalance the adversarial process. In other words, I could not count on a lawyer bringing out the other side of the story.

When it came time for me to give evidence, the trial was running ahead of time (quite unusual in my experience). I had to give evidence a day earlier than expected which meant that I had a rushed preparation, and had not considered the issues with any great preponderance. Another point to be learnt is to ensure that preparation is done early enough to deal with a case running ahead rather than behind time. Preparation is one of the most important keys for surviving court.

An unfortunate problem in the evidence base was that I had been asked to talk to the principal of the school about the child. The principal had been quite negative about the father's situation. On the day of the trial the class teacher, not the principal, was called to give evidence. Her evidence was favourable to the father and different to the principal's. The lesson here is avoid using external sources unless you know they will be cross-examined.

My survival in court depended on how I structured my evidence. Unfortunately, I made some errors in structuring the evidence in the report which became evident in court. In the report I was so struck with one particular incident the father had described, I had not considered detailing a number of lesser incidents. When the QC successfully shifted the main incident from the classification of psychological abuse to labelling it 'an inappropriate act', I was left in a precarious position. I had not documented enough evidence in my report to argue that there was a pattern of behaviour on the basis of one incident.

I compounded my problems by being too emotive. One particular statement I made created a lot of problems. I stated that a particular incident was "one of the worst examples of psychological abuse I had assessed in the Family Court". Unfortunately, by wording it like that, I was too emotive and when the court labelled the incident an inappropriate act, I was seen as extreme. Consequently, the importance of documenting patterns rather than just noting the extremes, as well as being emotively understated, became apparent from this experience.

The net result was that the judge had to resolve the difference between my report, the father's current evidence and the two other reports he had before him. From a judge's perspective, because of my emotive language, the most plausible explanation he had before him was the one proposed by the father's lawyer and that was partly the father was nervous at the time of the appointment and, more damaging for me, that I did not like the father. The concept of me not liking the father makes a lot of sense from a judge's perspective. As a psychologist who assesses rapists, murderers, drug addicts and all sorts of other 'undesirable' people, the concept of liking or not liking does not enter the equation. Therefore, my entire evidence was now viewed from the perspective of whether or not I had liked the person.

What I needed to be able to do in this particular case was present several other options for the judge. There were at least two other alternatives for the differences in our opinions. Firstly, the father had the benefit of reading my report and seeing my reaction. He was an intelligent man. The psychiatrist had made some notes about possible anti-social personality features, so I could have put forward the position that the father did present badly with me, realised his mistake and cleaned up his act on the shorter appointment with the psychiatrist. Alternatively, I could have argued along the lines that when I saw the father he was in an acute state of stress which suggested that he decompensated when stressed. Without either myself, or the unrepresented mother raising alternatives the judge accepted the proposition given by the QC.

A final aspect which I learned through this experience was that even though I had good quality contemporaneous notes, I wished that I had a tape recording of what the father actually said because it was argued that my notes misrepresented what the father had been trying to say. Subsequently I have considered setting up taping software to keep a verbal record of what is said to me so that if I am ever in the position of having to argue between what I found and what the person said, I can demonstrate my position.

When this case is examined as a whole, what started off as a seemingly cut and dried situation, ended up with a judgment which in essence said that I was swayed by personal feelings of dislike, put too much weight on other evidence which was found to be faulty, and that I was emotive. Ten years of conscientious report writing for the Family Court and a number of past judgments where I have been found to approach the task with objectivity and caution were potentially nullified in one trial. The irony in this case was that it was not even one where I saw the problem coming.

This case example highlights the underlying message of this book. How you set up your position, structure your evidence and prepare for court are of critical importance but court is like a game and even if you play the game to the best of your ability, it is not a game you will win every time.

Final Advice

The final comment I would like to present for your contemplation is that the process of court is only like a game, it is not actually a game. Court is one the cornerstones of our society and should be treated with the utmost respect. At the risk of playing semantics, you play the game of court; you do not play games with the court or the judge. The quickest way to have your evidence discounted is to present information which is not true or take a position other than that of assisting the court. After reading this book, I hope you can now play a better game, giving due respect to the dignity and importance of the legal system.

APPENDIX

Judge Wisbey – Draft Paper (2002)

It is with appreciation to Judge Wisbey that I include a copy of his draft paper on the expert witness and presenting expert evidence. Judge Wisbey of the District Court of Western Australia consented to this paper being included.

THE EXPERT WITNESS & PRESENTING EXPERT EVIDENCE

What is expert evidence?

In any trial, opinion evidence (that is the opinion of a witness as to the facts) is generally inadmissible. It is for the trial judge to draw all necessary inferences or conclusions from the evidence presented.

The difference between direct evidence of fact, and opinion evidence, correlates with that between lay witnesses and expert witnesses. Lay witnesses give direct evidence of what they have perceived with their senses, but are not permitted to express opinions; that is to express a concluded view based upon perception. Generally opinion evidence cannot be given by lay witnesses.

Opinions by experts are an exception to the general rule to which I have referred. Expert evidence "is admissible whenever the subject matter of the enquiry is such that inexperienced persons are unlikely to prove capable of forming a correct judgment upon it without such assistance, in other words, when it so far partakes of the nature of a science as to require a course of previous habit, or study, in order to the attainment of a knowledge of it".

In the psychological context it may be evidence of fact (the fact that the practitioner is able to demonstrate by appropriate testing that a person has certain intellectual disadvantages or that the testing reveals indicia of a recognisable psychological condition). The psychologist then draws inferences from the objective facts disclosed by psychological testing, and expresses an opinion which is able to be drawn because of that person's expertise or training.

There are three conditions that must be fulfilled before evidence can be received as expert evidence:

1. The person giving the evidence must demonstrate that he or she has the necessary qualifications to speak about matters the subject of the evidence. A witness cannot qualify as an expert unless his or her profession, habit, or a course of study or experience gives him or her a greater capacity of judging the issue than is possessed by other people. Once he or she has demonstrated the necessary qualifications, then he or she is able to offer opinion evidence (notwithstanding that in some cases it may be that the capacity is somewhat at variance with the qualifications).

2. The qualifications or expertise must relate to a matter which is capable of being the subject of expertise – that is of training and/or experience placing the person possessing it in a position to form an educated opinion on the matter not capable of being formed by persons generally. There is no scope for expert evidence in a situation where an unqualified person is capable of forming a valid opinion on the subject.

3. No expert is entitled to deal with a question, the answer to which ultimately depends upon the application of a legal standard, although this comment is easy to make but not so easy to apply.

Psychological evidence specifically

A psychologist in a personal injury case or a criminal proceeding can give evidence that he or she carried out an examination or testing of a person, and that the testing did or did not reveal any abnormality in the person tested. He or she cannot express an opinion that the tested person is genuine or malingering. The opinion must not extend to usurping the function of the trial judge in reaching the ultimate conclusion as to whether the person is truthful. That opinion is not admissible as the court is well able and required to draw the appropriate conclusion from the evidence presented.

The need to identify the basis of the opinion

The psychological evidence, to be of value, must indicate the base testing information forming the foundation for the ultimate conclusion, and that conclusion must be based as far as possible on objective fact.

In order to facilitate a proper appreciation of the opinion, and a sound evaluation of that opinion and its validity, it is essential the facts upon which the opinion is based are clearly identified. This then enables the application of commonsense and logic to be used to determine the validity of the opinion. The application of forensic logic should generally provide the answer.

It is important to indicate clearly in any report or in evidence, that part of the report or evidence that is based on ascertained fact, and that which is inferential (i.e. conclusions drawn from objective fact).

Evidential rules require that the facts upon which an expert opinion is based be established by admissible evidence. Consequently if an opinion is formed as to the nature and extent of a psychological condition, based in part upon the acceptance of material from another source, that material must also be proved by evidence.

Experience demonstrates that if, when preparing a report, the expert carefully identifies any condition precedent to the conclusions he or she has reached, it may provide an understanding of how and why other experts have taken a different view. Consequently it facilitates dialogue between 'opposing' experts and may contribute to an amicable and speedy compromise or resolution of the disputed issue. It also identifies the foundation facts, with the result that agreement may be reached as to those facts, and demonstrate that the forensic controversy is illusionary.

It is important to indicate the extent to which the conclusions reached are based on other material and/or an acceptance of the findings or conclusions of others.

The identification of an assumption of fact that might not be common to the expert contestants, may result in considerable reduction in the time taken up during evidence, and is clearly beneficial to all parties.

It is important that if and when a contrary view has been expressed, one addresses that view, identifying whether the difference is explicable by a difference of objective fact assumption, or is an inferential difference from the established facts.

The proper role of the expert witness

It is essential that the expert remain impartial to the cause, and appreciate that his or her obligation is to the truth (the court) rather than the party who has engaged them. The obligation is to present objective evidence.

In an article in the *University of Chicago Law Review*, the author noted that at the American Trial Bar expert witnesses had come to be known as saxophones, the idea being that the lawyer played the tune, manipulating the expert as though the expert were a musical instrument on which the lawyer sounded the desired notes.

In speaking about the tendency of experts to become partisan, it is important not to lose sight of the fact that a conflict in expert view, reflecting genuine differences of opinion based upon the then state of the psychological science, and perhaps reflecting the patients presentation, is an important part of the adversarial system.

It is important that the expert avoid adopting the role of a trailblazer for untried or dubious theories. If the expert wishes to be adventurous (and perhaps that shouldn't be discouraged) it is important that he or she enunciates clearly the novelty of the view, and identifies any opposing views.

The necessity to keep an open mind

A criticism of the adversarial system is that it discourages experts adopting a conciliatory approach thus narrowing areas of disagreement. The system also discourages experts from making concessions, once reports have been exchanged. There are very few of us who are not driven by ego, and the more experienced and senior we become in our particular area of expertise, the more difficult it becomes to recognise and compensate therefore.

Once an expert has given evidence-in-chief, he or she is reluctant during cross-examination to receive and accommodate contrary views concerned that it may be seen as a sign of weakness, or a lack of capacity. It is for that reason that an informal exchange of views prior to a trial is of assistance. If the expert is prepared to make himself available to address the concerns of each side prior to any hearing, there is a real possibility for accommodation of views.

There are often occasions when an expert, confronted during his or her evidence with material of which he or she was not previously aware, will not be prepared to acknowledge that it has any relevance or impact on his or her opinion. It is important that you are prepared to accommodate new material and to acknowledge that it impacts upon your opinion if that is the case. A witness should not be frightened to indicate to the trial judge that he or she would need time to reflect on the new material before indicating whether or not it affects the opinion that has been expressed.

Summary

When preparing a report or giving evidence it is important that an expert:

(i) set out fully the history provided by the client;

(ii) identifies with particularity the base material (factual assumptions) upon which the ultimate conclusion is founded;

(iii) be as concise and precise as the subject permits;

(iv) be as frank, objective and non-controversial as is possible consistent with professional obligation;

(v) does not reject an opposing view out of hand, but is prepared to consider and evaluate it with a view to distinguishing or accommodating it;

(vi) be conscious of the limits of his or her area of expertise and ensures that the evidence is contained by it;

(vii) be mindful of the fact that his or her obligation is to assist the tribunal of fact and not to usurp its task of determining the credibility of the litigant.

INDEX

A

adversarial system in courts 5, 79–80
   criticisms 133
affidavits 70
   in reports 71–2
agreed expert witnesses 16–17
anxiety management 115
appearance times, witnesses 104–6
appendices in reports 77
Australian Constitution *see The Constitution*
Australian legal system 3–5
Australian Psychological Society
   agreement with NSW legal practitioners 24
   ethical guidelines 60

B

balance of probabilities 88
best evidence rule 11
beyond reasonable doubt 88
bias *see* impartiality
breach of duty of care 40
briefings between lawyer and expert 106–7

C

case notes 47–8, 127
causation in negligence actions 40–1
client-practitioner relationship
   impact of legal process 26–7
   informed consent 48, 61
clinical assessment of clients, forensic assessment distinguished 25–7
clinical observations in reports 74
codes of ethics 38, 60, 61
codes of practice
   medical and legal professionals 24
   reports written for use in court 71
communication
   differences between legal and health professionals 1–2, 89–92
   jargon 91, 117
   see also language styles in reports
computer-generated interpretations of psychological tests 55
conclusion section in reports 76
conduct money 31
confidentiality 34–5
   counselling notes 101–2
   psychologists' reports 59–63
   risk management 48
   see also privacy
The Constitution 3
contract negotiation for experts required to attend court 118–19

copies of documents
 copyright considerations 35
 required in court 111
 required under subpoena 30
costs of attending court 30–2, 117–19
court attendance
 practical issues 103–28
 subpoena to attend in person 17–18, 29, 32–3
court judgments *see* judgments
court proceedings
 courtroom procedures 111–17
 customs and protocols 112–13
 dress standards 115
 etiquette 111–12
 rights of witnesses 113–14
 rules for non-legal professionals 6–11
 swearing in witnesses 81
 timeframes 7–9, 103–6
court-appointed expert witnesses 15–16
credibility
 evidence 9–10, 11, 63–7
 witnesses 10, 65–7, 71, 82–3
cross-examination 82–6
 feedback from lawyers 120

D

damages in negligence actions 41–2
demeanour of witnesses 114–17
destruction of case notes 48
direct evidence of fact, opinion evidence distinguished 129–30
disclosure 60–1
documents
 copies 30, 111
 copyright 35
 subpoena to produce 29–30, 34–6, 101–2
dress standards in court 115
duty of care 39–40

E

ethical standards 38, 60, 61
etiquette
 communication with parties 108
 court proceedings 111–13
evidence-in-chief 81–2
expert evidence
 admissibility 96, 129–30, 132
 conditions for receipt 96–7, 130–1
 presentation 10, 129–35
expert witnesses
 characteristics 100–2
 lay witnesses distinguished 129–30
 qualifications 96–7, 130–1
 role 98–9, 133
 witnesses of fact distinguished 27, 93
 see also forensic expert witnesses

F

factual basis of expert assessment challenge on cross-examination 85
Family Court rules of evidence *see Family Law Rules 2004*, rules of evidence
Family Law Rules 2004
 conduct money 31
 rules of evidence 21, 28, 55, 62, 71–2
feedback for improving skills as an expert witness 120–1
financial strategies, managing negligence risks 49–50
forensic assessment of clients, clinical assessment distinguished 25–7
forensic expert witnesses 13, 15–23
 treatment providers distinguished 24–5
Freedom of Information Act 1982 45

G

giving evidence 106–11
   avoiding defensiveness 115–16
   practical issues 123–8
government, source of power 3
GST (Goods and Services Tax), applicability 118

H

hearsay evidence 93–5
High Court of Australia, function and role 3–4
hired gun 68, 99, 102
historical material in reports 74
home offices, risks associated with 23
hypothetical scenarios when giving evidence 101

I

impartiality
   bias 18, 84–5
   challenge in cross-examination 84–5
   expert witnesses 133
   in reports 99
information sources relied upon 95, 131–2
   in reports 72
inquisitorial approach in courts 5
insurance, managing negligence risks 49, 50
introductory material in reports 70–1

J

jargon
   communication with lawyers 91
   use in court 117
judges
   assessment of evidence 10–11
   direct questioning of witnesses 87
   role 5, 56–7
judgments 10–11, 88–9
   feedback for expert witnesses 120
judiciary, source of power 3–4

L

language styles in reports 52–3
law, application to disputes 4–5, 7
lawyers, communication processes 1–2, 89–92
lay witnesses, expert witnesses distinguished 129–30
legal system, separation of powers 3
limitations to approach used in reports 73
literature *see* professional literature

M

materials for use in court 109–11
modifying reports 67–70

N

National Privacy Principles see privacy
negligence 14, 36–42
   see also risk management
notes to the parties in reports 62

O

objectivity see impartiality
opinion evidence
  admissibility 96, 129
  direct evidence of fact distinguished 129–30
  paper expert 18–19
  witnesses of fact distinguished 93

P

paper expert opinion evidence 18–19
party expert witnesses
  forensic experts 17–18
  treatment providers 25–7
peer reviews, managing negligence risks 46
pre-trial briefing of witnesses 106–7
pre-trial preparation 106–11
  costs 119
  practical issues 123–8
privacy
  balancing disclosure requirements 61
  complaints 34
  consent for case discussions 46
  implications of privacy legislation 45
  information in reports 48, 73
privilege
  claiming 35–6
  communications between lawyer and client 107
professional development
  reducing the risk of negligence 44–6
  skills as an expert witness 121–3
professional literature
  citing in reports 54–6
  questioning knowledge of in court 117
proofing witnesses 106–7
psychological evidence 57–8
  evidence of psychological testing 58, 131
  identifying basis of opinions 72, 95, 131–2
  use of computer-generated interpretations 55
psychologists' evidence, value in relation to other professions 83–4

Q

qualifications of expert witnesses 96–7, 130–1
see also credibility, witnesses
questioning techniques in court 116

R

R v Whitbread [case] 83–4
re-examination of witnesses 87
reasonable man or woman concept 37
reasonably prudent person concept 37–8
reasoning process, challenge in cross-examination 85–6
reasons for decision see judgments
referrals, managing negligence risks 46
reliable witness concept 78–9
reports
  guidelines for releasing 21–2
  writing for court purposes 51–77, 134–5
rights of witnesses in court 113–14
risk management 36, 43–50
  forensic experts 22–3
RRP *see* reasonably prudent person concept
rules of evidence 21, 92–5
  admissibility of evidence 130, 132
  reports 71–2
  see also Family Law Rules 2004, rules of evidence

S

second opinion expert evidence 19–22
service of subpoenas 34
skills development 121–3
standards of proof 88–9
Steffen v Ruban [case] 93–4
subpoenas 4, 17–18, 29–36
supervision, managing negligence risks 46
swearing in witnesses 81

T

taped case notes 47–8, 127
terms of reference in reports 75–6
test results in reports 74–5
   see also psychological evidence
testing the evidence 80, 81–9
therapeutic relationship see client-practitioner relationship
threats to subpoena 34
timeframes
   court proceedings 103–6
   for hearing disputes 7–9
timeliness when recording case notes 47
titles, use in court 113
treatment providers
   forensic experts distinguished 24–5
   issues associated with providing evidence 23–5
trial dates, setting 106

U

ultimate issue 56–9, 97
updating reports 67–70

V

verbatim notes see case notes
videotaped client interviews 4

W

witness expenses 30–2, 117–19
witnesses
   pre-trial briefing 106–7
   re-examination 87
   rights in court 113–14
witnesses of fact 93
   expert witnesses distinguished 27
   opinion evidence distinguished 93

REFERENCE LIST & FURTHER READING

Ackerman, M (1995). *Clinician's guide to child custody evaluations.* New York: John Wiley.

Australian Government Solicitors (2003, rev. reprint). *Australia's constitution.* Canberra: AGS

Australian Psychological Society Ltd. (1999). *Code of Ethics.* Carlton, Vic: APS.

Brodksy, S. (1991). *Testifying in court.* Washington: APA.

Byrne, D. (1986). *Cross on evidence.* Sydney: Butterworth Press. Current edition is Heydon, J.D., (2004). Cross on evidence, 7th edition Sydney: Lexis Nexis.

Champagne, A., Shuman, D. & Whitaker, E. (1992). Expert witnesses in the courts: An empirical examination. *Judicature, 76,* 5–10.

Cohen, E. (1995). *The law and the diving professional.* Santa Ana, California: PADI.

Davidson, G. (2002). Dealing with subpoenas. *InPsych, 24(5),* 31.

Faust, D. & Ziskin, J. (1988). The expert witness in psychology and psychiatry, *Science, 241,* 31–35.

Freckelton, I. R., Reddy, P. & Selby, H. (1999). *Australian judicial perspectives on expert evidence: An empirical study.* Carlton, Australia: Australian Institute of Judicial Administration Inc.

Garb, H. (1992). The trained psychologist as expert witness. *Clinical Psychology Review, 12,* 451–467.

Gaughwin, P.C. (2004). Beyond the noise and smoke: Some challenges for the mental health professionals entering the forensic area. *ANZPPL, 11 (1),* 44–49.

Kapardis, A. (1998). Psychology and law in Australia: An overview. *Law In Context, 16,* 106–117.

McCann, J. T. & Dyer, F. J. (1996). *Forensic assessment with the Millon Inventories.* New York: Guilford Press.

McNamara, B. (1999). *How Australia is governed: A simple guide to Australia's system of parliamentary democracy.* Fyshwick, ACT: CanPrint Communications.

Melton, G. (1987). *Psychological evaluations for the courts.* New York: Guilford Press.

Royal Australian and New Zealand College of Psychiatrists. (2003). *Ethical and practice guidelines #9: Ethical guidelines for independent medical examinations and report preparation.*

Sattler, J. (1995). *Clinical and forensic interviewing of children and families.* San Diego: Jerome Sattler Publishing.

Turncliffe, M & McBride, N. (2001). *Risky Practices.* Perth: Bayside Books.

Wetter, M. & Corrigan, S. (1995). Providing information to clients about psychological tests: A questionnaire of attorneys' and law students' attitudes. *Professional Psychology: Research and Practice, 26,* 474–477.

Ziskin, J. & Faust, D. (1995). *Coping with psychiatric and psychological testimony (5th ed.).* Los Angeles: Law & Psychology Press.

Cases
R v Whitbread (1995) 78 A.Crim.R 452
Steffen v Ruban (1996) 84 WN(Pt.1)(NSW) 264

Legislation
Family Law Rules 2004

Notes

Notes

Notes

Notes

Notes

Notes

About the Author

Dr Phil Watts is a well-known Western Australian clinical and forensic psychologist and is a past president of the WA branch of the APS forensic college. After completing a master's degree in Clinical Psychology in 1989, he worked for the Department of Community Development and Ministry of Justice before commencing a private practice in 1994. He runs a mixed practice involving forensic assessment and clinical treatment of families, adults and children.

A significant aspect of his practice includes running training programmes for various professions. Of particular note are his training seminars for lawyers and national training to health professionals on how to give evidence in court, report writing for court and assessment of risk in clinical practice.

With nearly 300 appointments as court expert in the Family Court, and over 500 reports for other courts, he is highly experienced in psychological assessment for court. He has given evidence in numerous trials in the Children's, Family, District, and Supreme Courts. An interesting peculiarity is that he actually enjoys giving evidence in court!

Additional copies of
a Reliable Witness
are available from:

Ogilvie Publishing
PO Box 1084
Canning Bridge, 6153
Western Australia

Phone: 08 9450 1618
Fax: **08 9450 8618**

Email: Philpsyc@iinet.net.au
Web site: www.drphil.com.au

The cost is $49.50
Plus $5.50 (postage and packaging within Australia)
(all prices are quoted in Australian dollars and include GST)

ABN 27 907 490 585